MEN, MUD AND MACHINES

More Achievements in Round Timber Haulage

Maurice H. Sanders

Cortney Publications

Published in 1987
by
Cortney Publications
57 Ashwell Street Ashwell Baldock Herts SG7 5QT

Reprinted 1990

ISBN 0 904378 35 7

Printed by Henry Ling Ltd, Dorchester

Contents

Acknowledgements

I wish to acknowledge my thanks and appreciation to the following friends without whose help this book would not have been possible.
To all the contributors who loaned photographs and gave unstintingly of their time.

To Howard Nunnick who is ever watchful of the Northern timber scene and sent me the photograph of the horseteam and Bedford Artic at Kendal.

To the Association of Professional Foresters, not for just inviting me to speak at their conference and the ensuing honorary membership, or the facilities at their demonstrations for my CORDA display, but rather the sharing in the rich fellowship that abounds among these current sons and daughters of our woods. My thanks goes especially to Pam and Mike Miller for their kindness to me.

To Martin Jackson of Hexham who spent hours on my behalf, culminating in a gathering of various old timbermen at an inn where photographs and yarns were pooled and sent to me.

To Sheila Morley whose editing has greatly improved the literary standard of this book.

To my good friend Ben, no other single person has done more for my publications than the indefatigable Ben Hinton. He alone tended and nutured the idea of another book and his efforts to make this possible has known no bounds.

To Jackie Hinton who undertook the marathon task of typing my rough text.

Any success I have enjoyed in writing must be attributed to my wife Helen, who patiently helps sort out the tangled thoughts I write, and my publisher Norman Gurney who occasionally winces at my expressions yet tactfully makes changes, acceptable to me, and palatable to the reader.

Not forgetting Miss Valerie Rice of Cortney Publications whose tremendous efforts have brought so much success to all my books, and Miss Celia Warren who splendidly masterminded the layout of my 245 photographs for me.

Sales of 'Stories of Round Timber Haulage' beyond my wildest dreams have been attributed to our many excellent Clubs and Societies and their rally field displays.

I am particularly aware of the efforts of Steve and Mrs. Wimbush — Commercial Vehicle and Road Transport Club.

Pat and Mrs. Treadway — Chiltern Branch Historic Commercial Vehicle Society. A whole host of young people who man the National Traction Engine Club bookstands and so many enthusiastic groups within the national Vintage Tractor and Engine Club. Then those fanatics of steam, Albert, Dave, Nigel and George, my super sales team at St. Mary's Mill, Chalford, Glous.

Please accept my most sincere thanks for a magnificent job.

The Photographs

The 245 photographs in this book are a major feature. Most of them have never been published, and most of them have been taken by amateur photographers, many of whom were in the "eighty-hour week brigade", and had no time to worry about posing refinements. Many photographs come from pre-war Kodak Brownie days. Delightful snapshots in themselves, which when enlarged magnify the defects, leading to many darkroom nightmares!

Some were rescued from dusty attics where they had been for 40 years or more; several were literally folded in drivers' wallets, and naturally the fold marks are reproduced. Where the reproduction is poor, it is because this may be the only copy of any one vehicle. This is not meant as a book of super photographs but rather of illustrations intended to give a better insight into the work and dedication of those wonderful men and women.

Almost by accident I found a gifted amateur photographer, Dave Gillow, who lives near me. The daunting task of copying this motley collection, containing dog eared, blemished snaphots, with thumbprints of Derv and coal dust, made him flinch a little. Reproducing some of the early cheap colour prints, now faded, took patience and skill but the end result is superb. Dave's artistry has brought you many a gem that otherwise would not have been seen.

Identification of some of the vehicles, particularly ex WD units, calls for your forbearance. One man had driven an outfit over three years and could still only describe it as a "a bloody big Yankee job".

Glosssary

APF — Association of Professional Foresters.

ANCHORS — A large spade or sprag mounted on the rear (generally) of a tractor to hold the machine whilst roping.

ARTIC — Articulated.

A CHANCER — One who cuts corners and takes chances, not long for this world.

BRIAR — A woodmans name for a cross cut saw.

C HOOK — A hardened hook shaped like a letter C used extensively until the advent of the hydraulic loader for quick fastening of a winch rope to a chain or sling.

CATS — Caterpillar Tractors.

CLEATS or SPUDS — Various metal bars that are fixed to drive wheels for extra traction in wet conditions.

COGS — slang for gears

CUBE — A cubic foot of round timber assessed by the use of the HOPPUS ready reckoner measure used by timber men for over one hundred years. Approximately 25 cubic feet of green hardwood weigh about a ton.

DED — Dutch elm disease.

DRUG — Another name for pole waggon or timber carriage.

EIGHT LEGGER — Eight wheeled lorry.

EGGLER — An egg dealer.

FERODO — brand of brake lining.

GRADIENT GLOW — The 'red hot' effect a steep hill had on some exhaust manifolds, and on brake drums descending same; most obvious at night!

GRUBBER or ROOTER — The process of grubbing up trees by the roots.

HCVS — Historic Commercial Vehicle Society.

KETTLE WEDGE — Name given to a wood chip axed out by fallers setting up a tree. (Ideal for firewood).

LODGER — The act of one tree falling into another when felling, in a big tree often dangerous to move. Frequently nicknamed "a widow maker".

QUAD — Light ex-army Gun-tractor.

SORTH — Stories of Round Timber Haulage.

SKIDS & 3 LEGS — Skids — wooden (preferably ash) support ramps used previously for loading; 3 legs or Shear legs previously used mostly in Wales and the North.

SNATCH BLOCK — Pulley for increasing pull.

SHEFFIELD BLIGHT — Description given to severely lopped tree. (Steel butchery).

TIDY STICK — Big tree.

TUSHING or SNIGGING — Term for extracting or pulling out trees to point of loading.

TWITCH — GIRTING IRON — WRISTER — WITTERING STICK — Local names given to a load binder that tensions loading chains in transit.

WIND THROW — A whole area of gale blown trees.

WOODPECKER — A poor axeman.

Health and Safety in Timber!

"Poor old Pete...dropped dead at the Mill ... only 44...heart they said...still, it was quick...a nice way to go...".

How many times have you heard that nonsense — or something like it? Why nonsense? I'll tell you: if Pete had been killed in a pile-up on the M6 nobody would dream of implying how lucky he was to have died in this way. Yet, struck down by heart disease, he is just as dead, just as quickly and — the greatest tragedy — years before his time.

Disease of the heart and arteries accounts for half the deaths in the U.K. The main killer is coronary artery disease which stops the supply of blood to the heart muscle itself; the effect is similar to a blocked fuel line, but rather more permanent in its effect! Like Motorway accidents, it is known to be largely preventable which ought to be of interest to readers of this book: HGV drivers appear to be particularly prone to it. More often than not, victims survive their first heart attack: that's the good news. If you're a trucker it can mean loss of licence, living, independence and self-respect.

CORDA — The Coronary Artery Disease Research Association — is researching into an "early warning" test to identify those of us most at risk of a heart attack before permanent damage is done and into ways of stopping the disease in its tracks. We've made exciting progress but we need ever-greater support from people like you who have most to gain from our success.

In the meantime, it makes sense to do all you can to cut down the risk of a heart attack. We are not much given to preaching at people but it does seem silly not to take good advice when its offered and our recommendations are:

Don't smoke — smoking is a major factor in causing heart disease.

Eat healthily — that means less of the 'greasy spoon' part of the trucker's diet; cut down *total* fats by as much as you can. It'll also help you lose weight if you need to. Remember - being overweight is a "risk factor" in itself.

Take regular exercise — but don't go mad; gentle exercise is the answer. Try taking the stairs instead of the lift; you spend a lot of your life on wheels — try walking a mile or two each week for a change!

Go easy on alcohol —more 'elbow bending' is not an acceptable way of taking extra exercise. Too much alcohol — however you take it — pushes up your blood pressure and that is *very* bad for your internal plumbing; and it damages the heart muscle itself! Limit yourself to about 21 units of alcohol per week (a "unit" is equal to ½ pint of beer or a single measure of spirits/ sherry or a glass of wine)

Avoid stress if you can — allowing yourself to get "wound-up" tends to raise — yes, the blood pressure again. However you do it: relaxation classes, thinking beautiful thoughts, talking-out your problems, etc. try to "cool-it". Don't let your worries be the death of you!

While your helping yourself to avoid a premature retirement or fatal heart attack you can rely on the fact that we'll be pressing ahead with our research just as fast as our limited funds allow. So when you next see a CORDA car-sticker — smile, because we — and our great supporters like Maurice are working for YOU! **Stay healthy!**

Anthony Burns
Executive Director
CORDA,
Tavistock House,
North Tavistock Square,
London WC1H 9TH.

In researching my book I continuously met old timbermen in their 70's and 80's who had wrestled with under powered, under braked, over loaded wagons up to 80 hours a week. Their counterparts today with super trucks in air conditioned silent cabs on air suspension seats with the law protecting their hours and loads have no such expectation of life. Hence my concern for these people!

Maurice H. Sanders.

Introduction

My grandfather was an Eggler, and quite late in life he bought and learned to drive a 30 cwt model T Ford lorry. My uncle Joe, who owned a similar vehicle for furniture removals, undertook the daunting task of instructing him. It seems the Ford would not heed verbal commands like "gee-up" and "whoa"! My grandfather took me, from the age of about six years, with him, at times often 35 miles away to deliver eggs in London. His negotiating of "Tally Hoo" corner, a busy North London junction, was as hairy as would be my attempt to cope with "Spaghetti Junction" today. Traffic was slower and cabs quite open, and various road users, particularly bus and taxi drivers, would shout critical remarks and judgments of each other's roadmanship. Grandfather frequently contributed with "how much blinking room do you want?" to anyone who got in his way.

The Ford main dealers at Beech Hill, Luton, sent out tickets for some "Ford Films", from the USA, to be shown at the local cinema — the Alma. That first visit to the flicks made quite an impression on grandfather and me. For a start our seats were much higher than those around us, until someone in the row behind explained the mechanics of tip-up seats! greatly improving our comfort, and their vision. I never see a "Keystone Kop film" without remembering that afternoon. Eyes glued to the miraculously moving pictures, each of us spell-bound as the camera cut from the train racing to a crossing, then to the usual Ford lorry over-loaded with chickens, doing likewise. A moment before the lorry was impaled on the Locomotive's cow catcher, grandfather, now living every moment, stood up and shouted loudly "look out!". I was too excited to be embarrassed, even when he endeavoured to discuss the merits of the accident with reluctant patrons around him.

An organist named Allender Fryer brought up the multi-coloured organ, which for me was, and still is, magic indeed. I believe this day had no small bearing on my life long love of cinema organs and lorries.

After 4 years apprenticeship in a Luton garage, I landed the plum job to operate one of the two wartime Priestman "Cub" dragline land drainage excavators that came to Eaton Bray. I enjoyed this occupation for 5 months until my call-up into the Royal Engineers in November 1941. I hoped 5 years in army muck-shifting had qualified me for a tractor driving job with the newly established National Institute of Agricultural Engineering Tractor Testing Division at nearby Silsoe in Bedfordshire. Armed with excellent references, I got as far as hearing "He's our man", but sadly my lack of educational qualifications out-weighted my practical experience. On the rebound I took the only driving job the Labour Exchange had, which was wrestling with a clapped out timber tractor at the local sawmill. They warned that five drivers had been and gone in four months. It was on this ferodoless beast, devoid of all brakes, that I learned my hauling craft, in spite of a few runaways. My love-hate relationship with Latil, and my life in timber had begun!

A caterpillar D4 winches out of one of Arthur Green's Leylands. No seasoned timberman is unfamiliar with scenes like this. When mud oozes up through the floorboards or stops you opening the cab door, then, and only then is your initiation into timber complete.
Courtesy Des Pickard.

Setting the Scene

This is a book of more achievements of men and women in timber. It is born of a flourish of feedback from people who not only enjoyed SORTH but identified with it. Over and over they said: "I laughed with 'em, I suffered with 'em, I lived every word", it became a common denominator far beyond the bounds of timber. Meeting you all was a great joy; pleasure, yes; and some even an honour. In fact this book of more amazing achievements, is a sequel about some of those people who read the last book.

The first record of any timber operation comes from the Bible. As I see it Solomon got in touch with King Hiram, "I've been going to build a temple for years," he said. "It's fairly quiet and I haven't many wars on, so now seems as good a time as any", he went on. "My folk are going to build it but it's no secret that no one can touch your chaps on felling and hauling". "Would you give me a price on loads of Fir and Cedar of Lebanon? "Bless the Lord", said Hiram, nipping off into the hills to price the job. Getting back to Solomon the following deal was struck. "I'll put in 30,000 men under my agent Andoniram" (who doubtless had plenty of whips to ensure productivity). "We'll fell the trees, run them to the coast and raft them. After that its up to your lads, and all I ask is that you feed my people". Hiram, already rolling in money, was in it for the prestige. There was no point in putting it in at so many shekels a cube ... and so it goes on in the first book of Kings, chapter V. It's all there.

Since old Hiram's time everything has changed and in some ways little has changed. True his manager had no computor controlled forward harvesters. Not one of the 9,000 AEC Matadors had left Southall, or had Andreas Stihl conceived his first chain saw, and today lashings are mostly verbal. But, even in my lifetime, men of timber have born the heat and cold burden of the day for a pittance which barely fed and clothed them. Few of this world's goods comfort their bodies, broken from chances taken in this tough cruel pursuit. When big elms were felled in Eaton Bray in the 1930's an old faller, named Cherry, laid rough in a bivouac of brushwood and was found half frozen to death, suffering from hypothermia without knowing the meaning of the word. In World War 2 lumberjills who operated iron seated tractors had to be treated for chilblains on the backside. Timber demands on flesh and limb are high, yet once it's in the blood few leave the profession. Remember, the word "Skidrow" comes from "Skidroad", referring to the shanty of logger communities out west as lumber jacks roughed out hard weather awaiting the opening of the "Skidding Roads".

The forest is a provider and killer alike. Workers are on a par with lion tamers. Become distracted, drop your guard for a moment and you may be maimed for life or worse. The chainsaw is a precision tool of these men's profession, not a fun machine hired on a Saturday.

The advent of the combine harvester had two profound affects on timbering. First, they required gateways twice the width. Few realise this had as much to do with the demise of purpose built short wheel base timber tractors, as has the lower price of the longer Matador that replaced them. Secondly, these prairie monsters required bigger fields. To make Britain self sufficient, grants to grub out miles of hedgerows were paid and over production was an unheard of word. This heralded a new breed of contractor with dozers, and expertise in rooting out big hedgerow hardwoods. Grubbers as they became known, combined muck and tree moving together, and something of my own experiences are set down.

I ceased timber hauling in 1953 and, with a monkey winch and early chain saw, commenced a land clearance business which I ran until I collapsed whilst felling a tree in 1984. I was another victim of heart disease. During a ten day stay at Brompton Hospital I was so appalled by the incidence of coronaries among young Heavy Goods Drivers that I started to raise funds for CORDA, the only charity funding the million pound plus heart scanner at Brompton.

During the 1950-60's I was honoured to be Youth Club Leader at Eaton Bray Methodist church for fourteen years. This was recently crowned by a mass return of ex-Club members who descended on Eaton Bray from far and near for a magnificent 'night of nostalgia'. My hobbies are theatre organs and my fifty year old Latil timber tractor. This puzzles my wife who recalls the days when the name Latil stood for frayed tempers and sprained wrists. Ill health robbed me of two years of schooling. I liked writing but my teacher would entertain the class by reading selections of my atrocious but well intended work, then throw it back across the class at me. Writing, therefore, is something that helps to keep me sane, rather than a gift or financial asset.

Most of all this is a book about more bluff, tough, valiant workers, a great cross section of achievers who have earned their place here. Men and women who have driven themselves and their machines up to and beyond the point of endurance. It has been a humbling privilege to meet more of these doyens of our trade. We shall not see their like again.

Wally and Old Bill

It was around midnight at the 'Dolly Varden' transport cafe Bagshot circa 1934. Young Wally Dell and his mate tucked into a steak and kidney pie, peas, taters and a mug of tea, all for one shilling and eightpence. Outside, 'Old Bill', a smart Sentinel Timber Tractor cooled off in the night air. She had just wended her way up from the Duke of Norfolk's estate at Arundel. Soon the crew would grease up, check the load, then disappear into the night with eighteen tons of timber steaming on up to Princes Risborough. At first light they would unload, then race back flat out at 12 mph to Arundel and a fresh crew would repeat the operation. Four times a week, by day and night, stopping once for coal and three times for water. On a good trip they made the eighty five miles journey in eight hours. Later an Artic did two four hundred cube loads a day.

This sets the scene for the life and times of these remarkable men and machines. It is interesting to note five men worked this job, one on a caterpillar pulling out, whilst the other four crewed the Sentinel in alternate pairs, ensuring 'Old Bill' never went cold. The whole wage bill for all five averaged fifteen pounds a week. Wally's long hours worked out at about four pence an hour. "It was the hungry 1930s and I was glad of work" he said. H Judd and Sons, Spencers Wood, Reading had the Sentinel in July 1930. Five only were built, four of which have survived. Tom Place of Northallerton, had an identical tractor at nearby Aldermaston.

Wally vividly recalled "Old Bill's" first day down at Lambourne. As third man, he helped pull out the 200 HP independently engined, winch rope, packed with grease, that plastered his smart breeches and leggings.

Sentinel's demonstrator stayed a week, but Wally was not allowed to drive until he was twenty one, and frequently was back working the horse teams. Later though he tells how they virtually lived on 'Old Bill', on the back by summer, in the cab by winter. That was not the odd night. We have all 'roughed it' in the cab and pocketed the night out money. These men really lived on the engine, day after day, once for three weeks on end. The driver slept slumped over the wheel, whilst the mate had added comfort of old coats laid on a plank. The catering facility was no less spartan. The men would stick a sweet tin with wire handle (for tea mash) down the boiler top chute. Remove the chute lid, turn the burner on a little for a nice easy heat and no dust. Bacon rashers were fried on the shiny shovel and tin lids acted as plates. Farmers supplied a drop of milk (mostly knowingly) dirty! hard! cruel! this was timber 1930's style. We never had any night out money at any time.

Among the marathon trips 'Old Bill' made were from Sonning, Berks to Marks Tey, Essex, always passing through London by night. Taking a sharp turn on one such run a forward butt pushed the side of the Sentinel in, when only a month old. Marshalls of Holloway, London was another venue for loads of walnut used on the famous ship 'Queen Mary'.

One big job was carrying six hundred cube on the specially made four twin wheeled trailer from Sherbourne, Dorset to Davenport Docks twice a week, finishing with a load up to Woolwich Arsenal at the week end. Work that out at under 12 mph! all before the day of the Log Book. They loaded by horses, Latils, and an early Holt tractor, equivalent to a Cat D 4. Transporting her called for considerable nerve. Odd times they would mount an old Foden lorry body on the bolsters, but mostly the drill was to put the trailer across the road with the rear wheels in the ditch. Then, with only two four inch planks chained to the shortened trailer and a ramp of cordwood, the Holt would mount her precarious perch, after many near disastrous attempts.

'Old Bill' weighed about eleven tons fully fuelled up, and Wally can name a few places not to take her!! Down by the river at Thatcham was one, where the trailer went in down to the bolsters one side and one could step off the load on to the ground with ease. They buckled up the stout anchor trying to rope out, much to the anger of Uncle Harold Judd. Being the Governer's nephew brought no favours for Wally. A unique system worked from Clifton on Teme, Worcestershire. A Latil ran a shuttle bringing the loads through to Broadway, using a spare trailer. 'Old Bill' would take the load on up the notorious Fish Hill to Claridges at Heythrop. But the days of steam were numbered. Wally's last job was grubbing roots in a park prior to ploughing in 1938. Finally this magnificent tractor went to the Metropolitan Water Board at Staines for pipe transport, and was not seen by him until years later on the rally field.

In 1986 at Rushmoor Steam Rally Aldershot, 72 year old Wally had the thrill and pleasure of taking 'Old Bill' round the ring as her driver gave the commentary.

In preservation 'Old Bill' is said to have carried out many recoveries. One such was a bogged excavator everyone else had given up on. It's calculated that the Sentinel exerted a hundred ton line pull freeing this machine. Wally left the family employ in the early wartime and eventually spent eighteen years hauling for T T Boughton of Amersham, where I first met him. He and a colleague called Rip Kirby (a humorous chap), had E R F artics and operated direct from their homes in Reading. Wally brought the very first load out of the massive Monksilver Somerset job of John Sadd's. Fifteen hundred tons of stone went into this impossible site, frequented by Sadd's own E R F which carried the back end 'piggy-back' style with the pole towering above the cab.

Harold Judd (by the door), Les Matchwick and Chas Woodley with 'Old Bill' in Maidenhead station yard in 1933. It took three days to fell this 1,000 cube oak, which was brought in 500 cube at a time.

Boughton artics trunked this timber up to Maulden Essex, all victims of the 'Cow Race'. The site entry on a steep hill was bad enough but up the top a farmer's cows crossed the road. Any driver caught after 'milking time' was bound to jacknife in the resultant sea of green slurry!!!

The Wally Dell story would fill a book. In fact it will. This great hulk of a man who would flip a binding chain over a load whilst others threw it, is writing it. Timbermen, especially those who remember steam, will 'live every word', but alas some will not even start to comprehend the life of this amazing man. Those, who unlike me, were not privileged to know Wally Dell and 'Old Bill'.

Wally, as many will remember him. Reg. HHU 491 ex-Ministry 5 Cyl. ERF, hauling a big poplar from Tiverton, Devon to Castle Hedingham, Essex.

Reg. HB 262 6 Cyl. ERF bound for Glenisters, High Wycombe.

Bill and the Mammoth

Greta Ewins of Henley-In-Arden, waited anxiously for news of husband Bill as he fought for his life in Coventry Hospital. Earlier that day, he and brother Peter had just placed the last long thin Oak atop a 750 cube load out at Atherstone. Cautiously Bill had coaxed out the rope, eyeing the tree most likely to roll, but it didn't. Four others did though, just as he prepared to throw the binding chain. In a moment Bill was crushed between the load and the Matador jib, and helplessly Peter eased the tractor forward and released the gory mess! The medical report brought little cheer. For starters he had sustained severe kidney damage, internal bleeding, as yet unstemmed, untold spinal injury, and more to come. The doctor said if he pulled through, one thing was certain, he would never work again. That was November 7th, 1960. It is believed good nursing and previous superb bodily fitness featured most in Bill's return to hauling in just 3 years.

After War-service timberman Father Ewins had all 4 sons with him at various times, starting out with ex W D Quads. But it was brother Alf who teamed up with Bill until Alf emigrated to Australia in 1974 when Bill became his own man.

Bill hankered after a purpose-built machine and went to "Oates of Worksop" buying their well worn old Unipower (jammed in low ratio) and Crane 4 wheel trailer for £250.00 the lot. After the long trip home at 12 mph, Bill himself stripped out and fixed the intricate transfer box, for all time. Spurred on with the "real Macoy" at last, these 2 lads in their young enthusiasm went out and put 600 cube (I ask you!) on this 4 wheeled trailer to try it! and try it it did! Suffering brake fade down a hill, they charged into a front garden performing a super knife which cut the cab top off at bonnet level, as clean as a whistle. Both lads had doubled down on the floor as they saw themselves approaching and going under their own load from the side! all on one summer's evening. Removing the mutilated draw-bar, Bill says the local blacksmith "tidied it up a bit!" and by midnight the beefy load was winched free of the bungalow it threatened. Recoupling to the now topless Unipower, undeterred the boys were now back on the road again, when joined by the local bobby who despairingly enquired — "What ever are we going to do with you Billy Ewins?" "See us home for a start" came the reply. "What! not without lights" queried the friendly officer. However the Ewins' cheek and charm prevailed, and following in the PC's car headlights the unlit load rolled on in utter darkness. So much for Bill's love-affair with Unipower.

Soon he was in Bird's scrapyard eyeing another cheap winch. Boss-man Tom Bird offered good advice — "You want tackle that can realise your ambitions" he said, leading Bill to an immaculate Matador, newly painted and lined out in gold. It had a matching heavy low-loader, offered at £1,000 complete, due to lack of work. With a sickly laugh Bill said "If pigs had wings, they would fly", resenting Tom's pointless remark. But Tom insisted — "Go home, and come back with every penny you can lay your hands on". Almost for a laugh, Bill did and returned with £200 and diminished hopes! "That's fine" said Tom who had tested Bill enough. "Now drive the Matador away, it's yours, I will find you some work, and you pay me the rest as you can". In fact a good old-fashioned 'Gentlemen's Agreement' had been struck. Running timber down into Wales and returning with steel for Tom, paid well. Then every weekend Bill worked for Birds, picking up scrap Transformers on the low-loader all over the country. One of the first was in Bristol, and Bill flinched as the low-loader sagged on reception of its sudden burden via one of Sparrows big red cranes. "What have I got on there?" Bill asked the driver, who said with a cursory glance "about 40 ton", which, with the trailer, grossed at about 50 ton.

Undaunted they made for the Midlands, in FWD low ratio, Bill's arm working like "a fiddler's elbow" as he used the bottom end of the gearbox, leaving ruts in the tarmac, scrubbing the chevron tyres on many a hill! Every weekend was committed to Birds, until the deal was honoured, an important matter to Bill, who loved a challenge. As he was to find, the world of timber had plenty of those waiting for him.

This was the first of many Ewins' Matadors. Bill loved the day of the Mat and Drag (his name for a pole-trailer). The New Forest was the scene of an early rough job. Hauling soft woods up to Ivans of Rugby, seven hours up, unloading by himself, five hours back! All loaded after dark with the Mat's rear working light often up to 11 o'clock. "In mid-winter, in a leaky living van, when the blankets froze to the side of the van, and you set off at 2.00 am just to try and get warm, as we often did — that's what you can call slogging it for a crust" said Bill forcefully. One favourite Mat had her 7.7 engine replaced by an 11.3 AEC unit — "she ran like a train" enthused Bill. High speed diffs enabled 49 mph. Many a modern trucker looked twice when a 40 year old Matador loaded sky-high with logs over-took him on a hill. "Did they make a good job of fitting the 11.3?" I questioned. "They, They who's They?" said Bill pulling me up sharply. "It's me not they. I adapted that, and do my own engineering".

A Police Sergeant waved Bill down outside a Cotswold "Cop-Shop" and listed complaints from motorists, daily obstructed by long impassable loads. "If the customer wants 'em long, I haul 'em long, he's paying" said Bill. By now they had been joined by a keen young Constable with a tape measure who claimed it was just 112 feet from the "red rag" to the Mat's front bumper. "I'll go and fetch the book that explains this type of offence" he said, knowing this must be a cert! Humouring the Officer, Bill enquired what he'd better do? With a wink and a wave, "push off" he was urged "before he comes back with that book!" Time after time the police gave us the benefit of the doubt, not that there was much in this case!

Up to now, Bill had little time for the "clean shirt and sun-glass brigade". His description of Artic drivers, whose wagons were loaded by others, accounting for their smarter appearance. But in 1967, his first Artic unit was an AEC registration number ERF 759E. However, it was the legendary 6 × 4 AEC Mammoth Major registration number UNX 147G that had compelled me to seek out this doyen of our trade. Three different folk had told me about a massive 1,200 cube Bill had taken into Pontrilas Sawmills. Bill looked puzzled and honestly could not recall the event. "You have to remember such a load" I insisted, but Bill explained he always put 1,000 cube plus on this outfit anyway. She had brought 1,100 cube of wet Beech (say 22 cube to the ton) up from Devon, all across the moors time after time. "A fantastic wagon, which I kept for 5 years and did 250,000 miles with her", he justly boasted. She had one small behavioural quirk! When loaded, the double drive would tend to cause her to travel straight on when cornering if one failed to drop a cog or two! A consideration we must allow this noble beast. "Ah, a good load" Bill's face lit up with the memory. "I put a fair load of long Spruce on at Burton-on-Trent (with the extra long pole unit we made up, I could take 75 footers with ease). Bound for Henry Gould's of Fazley, I just squeezed under a 16 foot railway arch, clearing off all the underside moss for British Rail." Out on the road, Bill waited for Gould's to clear the decks for this ginormous intake, while the office checked the tree numbers and measures. An astonished veteran appeared and announced "Bill we've checked this load and you've got 1,540 cube on". "I must have!" agreed Bill nonchalantly. In the early days Bill was often booked for over-loading. He admits it doesn't pay then added ruefully, "but then nor do legal loads either".

A tough challenge came in the form of a big time penalty job. 50,000 cube of mixed hard-woods at Christmas Common, Bucks, to Wragby, Lincs, a 300 mile round trip. Could he deliver fast, the client wondered? "Can you take it if I do?" came the reply. Well Bill could and they couldn't, until another crane was hired to meet the deluge of Ewins' timber that poured in. Bill put his own 3 sets of tackle and 2 on hire. He tushed, sawed, measured and loaded every cube himself. Five loads a day left the site. In pairs the first two left at 2.00 am, the next at 5.00 am, the last at 7.00 am. Alf would be back for a late dinner in the van — it all ran like clockwork. "It's the planning that counts" said Bill.

The Ewins' tenacity and love of a timber challenge accounts for a lot of jobs that have beaten others. Like a large Wellingtonia Fir in a park. In half an hour it was loaded, bound on, and there was time for a snack. Eyeing the "Mammoth" a gamekeeper remarked "So you've got it on then!" "Why not?" chorused the lads. "Three other different sets of tackle have tried and given up on it" knowingly replied the old chap.

The "Mammoth", who it was calculated earned more than twice as much as any of the others, was finally traded for a L reg Foden. An unfortunate vehicle that brought nothing but trouble and was nicknamed "The Pain". Being rolled on route to Bishops Castle, Salop, didn't help either, but the driver survived would you believe!

Moving with the times, Bill's next choice was a Magirus Deutz 8-legger. Bill Ewins was the first man in Britain to put a 15 ton metric Highland Bear into round-wood haulage. This self load outfit was excellent for the right job! "So it met the Ewins' demands?" I queried. "Well it ran regularly from Henley-In-Arden, across to Cromer in Norfolk, loaded, then back over to Venables of Stafford and home. That was a 160 mile round trip a day, and wasn't bad" Bill said thoughtfully, then added "She kept up with Bubbles (her driver) and there is not much wrong with a wagon that can do that!"

In 1984, 60,000 cube of prime hard-woods came up for sale near Oswestry. Most potential buyers lost interest as the impossibilities (for ordinary hauliers) of extraction were revealed. Bill walked and waded the job with the would-be client, who asked if Bill could move the hard woods. There was one way, and only one way out. It was over a 100 yard wide bog, beside a river which had to be crossed twice. Bill's requirements were at least 20 tons of stone for each river bank, to ramp up out of the water. It took 100 tons of cord-wood to build a wooden causeway across the bog, this was all fetched, carried and consolidated with Bill's D50S Komatsu loader. The wettest part of the bog was drained by a big hollow tree winched into place, thus forming a natural culvert. The Volvo tractor units were on good terrain. The trailers, 2 or 3 most days, were taken in and brought out with a Matador equipped with a fifth wheel coupling. "Could the Mat cope fording the river with water well up her 1400 × 20's?" I questioned. "With my big Cat pulling her and a 20 ton Komatsu pushing up the back end, how could she fail?" said Bill

Greta and Bill Ewins with their girls, and the first new AEC in 1967.

Motorists complained to the Police about Bill's long loads. Add the length of this AEC Militant and one sees why.

The legendary 6 × 4 AEC Mammoth Major. With extended long pole she carried seventy five footers in comfort. This vehicle covered 250,000 miles in five years and regularly had loads of 1,000 cube. Bill said it was the finest wagon he ever had.

Would you believe the driver got out and walked away!

with a grin.

On the wall in their home, I admired an almost life size painting of a Jack Russell terrier. "That was Polly" said wife Greta. "It was Bill's little cab dog, killed when a tree fell on her." "So, what's it like being married to this 'Latter-day Henry Giles'?" I asked. "Where do I begin?" Greta replied. "There is all the paperwork on our 3 outfits, and 2 or 3 on hire at times; all the invoicing, plus tracking the timber we haul on contract against that Bill buys, sells and hauls; fetching and carrying, be it a wheel out on the M6, or spares to a breakdown scene; holding spanners and bars in the workshop; bringing up 2 children was almost a side-line — I don't know how I did it!" (words I've heard so many times). In fact under pressures like these, Greta had succumbed, and had a nervous breakdown, but that's all behind her now. As we talked of the accident rate in timber, Greta referred to the emotional casualties. "All our drivers have had divorces" she said, recalling phone calls from irate wives. Bill's policy of an early start and late finish has scorched many a dinner and relationship.

Bill Ewins is making noises about "packing-in", and in fact down Gloucester way, they are laying bets on the chances. I doubt this "Warwickshire Warrior" will easily quit the excitement and challenge of the woods. Who else will tackle the jobs that others won't? This man has shifted a hell of a lot of timber, since the Medics said — "He would never work again".

WHOOPS! These Volvo bumpers soon pull off. Somewhere in Derbyshire.

The penalty job of 50,000 cube at Christmas common that went like clockwork.

The lads stop for maintenance. This AEC Matador was beefed up with a 11.3 engine. Notice how Bill mounts his jibs amidships.

Maggie runs off the road.

When ever Bill took this 20 ton Komatso back to the yard, he reckoned to bring home a bit of firewood.

Just on 900 cube in this elm. Loaded one end at a time with a Matador and Bray Loader lifting together.

Worcestershire Whistlestop

Of the dozens of folk who bought my book through Ben Hinton, several "old-timers" expressed a desire to meet me. Basing my camper van at his home, a most exhausting, but enjoyable and ego nourishing itinerary was adhered to. Loaded with tapes, film and valium, my first stop with stocks of books was at the excellent Costwold Countryside Museum at Northleach. Formerly a House of Correction and a Police Station in the 1950's where yours truly had spent a night in a cell!

I was hauling from Somerset to Hampton-in-Arden one summer's evening when tired, impatient and stuck behind a farm tractor, I "dropped a cog" to pass quickly. The ERF in my charge reared up, as was its wont, and bang went a half-shaft right outside this house of law on the Fosse Way. I rang for a spare, lit a red hurricane lamp and prepared for a long night in the cab. I cringed as the Sergeant eyed my over-loaded unit, but he had brought out food, not his book, and said "We have a room for you with blankets in there. I'll not lock the door lad" he assured me.

Ben had a few days hols, and met me on the A40. We wended our way up to our first call in Cranham Woods. Reg and son Jim Hannis, are farmers and timbermen, growing straw for thatch and cutting a bit of timber, in a Mill out of this world, in more ways that one. I adjusted to Reg's droll humour as he showed me round. His 15 cwt Chev was offered him for £100. "Throw in that, and we have a deal" Reg had said to the vendor, pointing to a rough old ex-council Morris Commercial Tower wagon, that became a form of mobile scaffolding.

Cranham legends include old Bill Price who, in the War, clear felled acres, for a shilling a tree, big and small alike. Near here, in an horrific accident, two lumberjills lost an arm each, wrestling with a buckling two-man chainsaw. One buxom land-girl strode the furrow with a horse plough towed by a Fordson on spade lugs. The farmer, looking back at the land-girl's ample thighs, was so distracted that he drove over the headland, through a stone wall, turned in the road and re-entered the field via the gap without stopping. On one occasion Reg waved down a speeding Quad on a hill, to warn of a road blocked by a lorry and car interlocked together. "We'll soon shift em with this" they said, and did, but not with the winch, but front bumper, ploughing through an opening for the waiting traffic, as on-lookers stood by aghast.

Red House Farm Sawmills is a great music making centre. On Tuesday evenings when Reg and Jim, both collectors and adept players of vintage Melodeon (members of the Accordian family) gather like-minded friends. The rafters of the workshop ring as music and cider flow freely. Regular engagements come from W.I. parties to the "Black Horse Inn", such is the fame of this group of people who know the real meaning of home entertainment. Reg who had just come off the bandmill, banged the dust off his cap, then delighted me with the "Winster Gallop" like a pro. I found no signs of affluence in this place, but a great quality of life; the two are inseparable. Mind you, digging one's self out each winter is part of the price to pay to live in this lovely spot.

Ben takes the wheel of Reg's ex-RAF David Brown. Scores of these tractors became popular for threshing and timber hauling.

This little 15 cwt ex-WD Chev has given Reg long and faithful service.

Currently serving the mill is this 4 × 4 ex-WD Ford.

Reg gives me a tune in the workshop, where the rafters ring and cider (strong enough to free rusted bolts) flows on a Tuesday night.

Jack Timberell

Seeing a rabbit disappear down a hole in Cowley Woods, Glos, gave Charles Dodgson, alias Lewis Carroll, the idea of "Alice in Wonderland". However, there was nothing diminutive about the huge trees there, or Jack Timberell of Winchcombe who felled 43 acres of them.

After army service, felling big trees became Jack's speciality. He's a big man who likes a big challenge. His ideas for modifications on the early Danarm two man chainsaws became standard as he pioneered big cutting work for them. Among his achievements was a 500 cube Elm butt at Sudeley that contained an ingrowing arrow head, which rather dates it. Later, with his son-in-law Joe, they worked on a host of big jobs, and many a tree was cut really at ground level for which they received an extra 10 shillings a tree. At Sudeley Castle, on the banks of the Issbourne, (one of the few rivers that runs north) they had a big fall of Poplars, planted seventy years ago by a local man still alive in 1986. Robert Wynns hauled some of the big trees, and one such, laid at the rear of Tewkesbury Abbey. Turning out of Gander Lane, they had just inches to spare at the top of the road where there was a locked car ahead. The crewe of the F.W.D. and Jack, all hefty lads, half bumped, bounced and carried the car clear, shearing the bumper bolts in the process.

Jack's masterpiece is his own designed and built power-fork and loading grapple. It is the ultimate in resourcefulness as one would expect from an ex Royal Engineer.

Just down the road at Stanway we called in to Cliff Brownlow's yard to see his ex Turriff Construction Reo 6 × 6. Cliff had re-engined the vehicle with Bedford diesel. A hard-working well-built working motor this, at Cliff's busy little Mill.

We'll never see elm like this again. Felled at Lechlade.

This massive elm stood behind Tewksbury Abbey, and presented many problems but Jack was undaunted. Big trees were his speciality.

One of Wynn's FWD's, and the lads who bumped a bumper off a parked car.

A very tight fit in Gander Lane, Tewksbury. One uncalculated move on turning out of the lane could have demolished the fronts of these frail cottages.

A big elm, on Lord Banbury's Estate, cut clean, level and low. Jack and son-in-law Joe dropped these large trees like 'ninepins'. Circa 1970's.

Jack loved his dog. Many other fallers had a dog. Not just for the odd rabbit, but when the forestry commision paid a shilling a tail to combat the grey squirrel menace a sharp dog earned good beer money.

Cliff Brownlow with his gorgeous REO 6 × 6 at his industrious little Sawmill, Stanhay, Glous.

Cats Galore

Ron Morgan who helped so much with SORTH had passed away. His son Roger and his wife Anne entertained us at their Broadheath home, just across the Common from Sir Edward Elgar's birthplace which is now a museum of his memorabilia including the name plate of the Locomotive called after him. The gaunt figures of dead trees are said to have inspired his more sombre works. Perhaps being spared the ravages of Elm disease in his day accounts for the lighter, brighter music that issues forth creating an uncanny presence throughout the cottage, that overlooks his beloved Malvern Hills. A surprise was marked next on the itinerary, and it was kept so, as Roger hurtled us 40 miles up the M5. Not until we swung into the old Bowmaker Factory, now Finnings Limited, Cannock, was all revealed. Acres of tracked and wheeled machines produced a hue of Caterpillar yellow as far as the eye could scan. As yellow as the Valium tablet I slyly took, to subdue the, then, eminent excitement. Now not for Roger were the joys of timber haulage. After spending 3 years at Worcester Technical College, he served a 5 year apprenticeship at Hennan & Froude of Worcester. He then spent another 10 years there as an engineer specialising in Dynamometers — a word I can neither pronounce, spell or describe even! but I gather when coupled to a test engine and put under load, it measures torque reaction which when multiplied gives you horse power! Roger's own company has rebuilt and serviced these vast machines for 8 years.

In the Finnings' test shop one 475 h.p. Cat Dump Track Engine was running on a hydraulic Dynamometer capable of 4,000 h.p. It was breath-taking as Harry Harper, who is in charge of the Unit, showed us around. Ben, of course who has tested many a Foden engine the other way! wanted to see the Cat 3306 engine bound for current Foden trucks. Ex Corporal Harry (4 years with the Royal Engineers) showed us over this heart of "Caterpillarland". I've got news for any as long out of touch as I am. Those b..... starter ropes and D4 donkey engines have long since gone! No seat cushions to upturn from overnight rains. Now exist super luxury cabs, air conditioned, heated, with side window wipers, containing electronic monitoring that first warns, then shuts down on a serious mal-function. I saw the wheeled Cat 910, the darling of the "big North West" USA where, fitted with massive hydraulic 24 inch shears, nothing is chain-sawed under 2 feet diameter with her around. The D9L at 52 tons (less equipment) towered above us 12 feet 6 inches to the cab top. Whatever would old Uncle Ben Holt the founder, have made of all this? The great Cat D11N at 770 h.p. on the way, leaves me speechless as did the organisation of this rare treat, courtesy of Mr Alan Godsall of Finnings Limited.

The story is told, that when Ben Holt got bogged with a wheeled tractor, having to walk in mud for help, taking one step forward and slipping back two, he said it was like 'a hoss on a treadmill'. That gave him the idea of wheels driving in a track. In 1905 he claimed his first track laying tractor, 'ran over mud like a caterpillar'.

Broadheath for me will always mean my kind of music, not only Elgar's but that chorus of great Cat machines, singing in concert, conducted by young technicians. But as an ageing sentimentalist none of them ticked over as sweetly as the old 3 cylinder D6! but you reader are far too young to remember that music, surely?

Ron Morgan (see Sorth Page 77) with one of our trades ubiquitous AEC Matadors. What other forty five year old ex-WD vehicle, in good order, would fetch £3,000 in 1987? Incidently the army winch load classification is 7 tons not seventy, as some of you seem to think.

'God's Perfect Man' – Ben fetched this 300 cube beech from Bradwell, Glous. on the 10th November 1986. Bill Jefferies, (by the trailer) in the pouring rain, drove out with his Fordson Major, fell and corded up this tree alone. He is known to be in his mid-eighties. Some say older. Bill says 'God only made one perfect man, and I see him every morning when I shave'.

The Shropshire Lads

A wall of Alf Corfield's home in Easthope near Much Wenlock, is bedecked with trophies, cards, plaques, cups, a barometer, a beautiful clock and 7 gold (3 A's) medals. Although a champion tree-man, these are awards of his hobby — athletics and Alf has always loved sport. In 1921 aged 21, he went to Harrods of London to buy the finest bamboo vaulting pole, price 50 shillings (about 2 weeks wages for a farm worker then). Ben and I winced as this lad of 86 summers gave a demonstration run, with that very pole, up his garden. His record was clearing 12 feet, landing on his feet, unlike on the air cushions of today. Prizes for 100 yard races, until he was 50, came from Crewe, Coventry and Ironbridge. But pride of place goes to a medal presented in July 1986 inscribed "Alf Corfield Oldest Athlete, 100th Olympic Games Medal".

Reg Reece, Alf's half brother, a mere 72 year old, started felling at 17 and produced some wonderful snapshots taken with his own Box Brownie No 2 camera. Alf though, started at 14, working with his uncle, when lodging money was 9 pence a night and they felled for a farthing a cube.

Later, Reg and Alf, with one or two lads of their choice, contracted mainly to W J Claytons Birmingham, John Hickmans Wolverhampton, and Jabez Barker Shrewsbury. They travelled across Wales and down to Buckinghamshire. But most woods the length of the Cotswolds in Gloucestershire, down to the Bristol Channel, have rung to the blows of the 7½ lb Elwell axes used by these professionals. They push-biked hundreds of miles until Reg bought a distinctive Scott (water cooled) motor-cycle and side-car for his 8 foot cross-cut American Atkins Saw, and sundry kit. For the same purpose Alf gave £90.00 for a BSA three-wheeler car of which one timber merchant would joke, on settling his account, — "Now you can get that other wheel for your motor!".

Many a horse, and man, has been killed "in timber". Referring to a great strong Shire, Alf said, "Old Digger dropped dead with heart failure". Down near Burford, two horses were considered enough to pull a tree leaning over the road. But taking the strain so long left them spent when due to pull, and this big Beech went back across the road. The two exhausted creatures were pulled writhing into bushes, the one nearest the snatch bloke floundered hopelessly as the taut collar throttled him. The harness was cut in the nick of time, but the animal was never used for tree felling again.

If there is a big limb on the side of a tree and if the tree falls on this limb it can split and ruin the tree, or at best "shake" the grain fibres. Consequently any such limb would be 90% chopped through to break on impact. Reg described the acquired skills of balance, to stand aloft and "axe out" both sides for perhaps 2 or 3 hours on a big awkward branch. Similarly, chopping out back hanging limbs, Alf has spent half a day up a big tree, having both his dinner and tea passed up on a rope. Brandishing a trusty pair of climbing irons, made to measure by a blacksmith in 1930 for 10 shillings, Alf told how he climbed 60 feet to fix a special 300 yard long cable for Brunsdons of Stonehouse Foden, pulling across a hill. Interrupting my comment Alf said "But I've topped that many a time. One fallen tree measured to the point I have worked was 85 feet!" One of his lads had fallen 45 feet, and these veterans of the woods described vividly how they knocked a hole in a high dry stone

The bark peeling gang employed by Alf's uncle. (third from right) at Iron Bridge. Circa 1915. Oak bark was used for tanning and peeling was a most exhaustive task.

wall for access to the ambulance stretcher. But Alf had no irons in 1918 in the army. A bullying Sergeant picked on the wrong man when he pointed to the barracks flag pole saying "Get up there". This Alf did, shinning to the top with ease, where he sat on the pole cap, and remained there for the rest of the parade.

Much of their timber was axe-felled, and today folk, who have never seen let alone used a sharp 7 lb axe, talk about chopping down a tree with a chain-saw. I always love to ask how one chops with a saw! Well these men really did fell without any kind of saw. When cutting in the directional "Fall" or "Throat" required perhaps two of you striking alternately bringing in the axe blows almost horizontal at ground level, standing legs apart knees and back well bent fetching out chips the size of big pasties for an hour or two, sorted out the men from the boys.

In 1932, one big Oak on the Kinlet Estate had 600 cube in the first length, and it was bought for church restoration work for £135.00 and sent to London hauled by a Foden Steamer in one lump. Special insurance was taken out on all the road culverts, and an insurance claims man checked every crossing of this marathon load.

During World War II, Alf employed 10 women who made good money cutting 16,000 pit props. One lady now of 89 years, recently reminded Alf of those days. "Another buxom wench, broad on the beam, had buttocks (my word not Alf's!) like a hop sack, but my, how that gall cut timber!" he said smiling.

Their first chain-saw was a Teles-Smith which Alf often pulled out of the cut, because he could chop faster! Later, sons John and Peter joined the gang. From a recent photograph of a big Beech tree felled and trimmed out by Peter, the old adage "Like father like son" rings true.

Not until 1983 did Alf retire from tree work. Sixty-nine years of true professionalism lie behind this remarkable man, who still drives his car, does not wear spectacles, and has never taken a pill until hospitalised last year. A man who attributes long life to keeping fit, hard work and being contented with his lot.

These two men have run well their life's race in timber. They have finished the course, and passed on their craft to others who will not easily fill their shoes. We shall not see their like again!

Sadly Alf died before this book was published. At the funeral service, as a tribute, extracts from his story were read to the congregation; an act the author found touching.

An early felling scene at Ledbury. Alf's vivid memory brought recognition of all this group, including the measurer rod in his hand. Note the wicker cider basket beside the tree. 'Working face to face these men soon set up a big tree', said Alf.

Brewing up at Colwyn Bay – that's Dick with the kettle, he always made the tea in the kettle. There's me with the loaf of bread and that's Charlie Russell in the middle. A great axeman was Charlie, Alf explained.

Perched 35 feet up this tree, Reg axes a big limb for two hours to prevent a split, when this tree fell at New Radnor. Chopping beside the toes and missing them, and keeping balance for two or three hours was part of these men's skills.

Tag-sawing at Kinlet – when a tree was so big, even a long crosscut saw had limited travel. A length of twine gave extra pull from two second men.

May 1st 1936 is scribed (carved) on the log. Alf's gang pose at Bloxly, Glous. Naming each man's special skills. Alf said, "These men were real timber cutters".

Langley Park, Slough, 1933. Another tagsaw job.

Douglas Clayton, Timber Merchant, at the foot of the 600 cube Kinlet oak. Alf climbed up this tree forty feet, with irons, to cut the first limb.

Reg. UDA 513 the 1957 Douglas Logger Type 4 that I later owned and ran through the 1970's. The lad by the wheel is Peter Corfield who has taken over from his illustrious father.

JUX 135 pulling a lime tree for Alf. This ex-Jabex Barker 6 × 4 Forden is now beautifully restored. Driven by its owner, Lionel Amos, it completed the HCVS Brighton run in 1987.
These photographs are courtesy The Ben Hinton Collection.

The Robert Jones Car

"Get her knickers off. I need the elastic", Robert Jones instructed his wife from under his broken down car. To this day daughter Vivien Mason never knew how the elastic was used, but it got them home.

Before she was born in Suffolk, her father a young aspiring engineer in Kensington London gave much thought to building himself a light car in 1923. The idea was for it to be less than 8 cwts to beat the taxation weight limits. The result was a three wheeler registered 'The Robert Jones Car'. A fascinating write up to a motoring journal was in his papers after his death. The base unit was a model T Ford with its 23 h.p. engine slimmed down. The cut short chassis had a single chain driven rear wheel. The gears, including a reverse, were housed in a gearbox turned and made from hardwood by the designer. Aluminium front wings and a ⅝″ match board body completed the 'R J' as it was known. She ran like a bird, but was just over weight until Bob drilled umpteen holes in every part safety permitted. Power, comfort, speed, reliability, it had the lot. In fact, whenever he parked up, questions about the origins of this hybrid's pedigree was the only annoyance. The 'R J' ran

The Robert Jones (T Ford engined) car that served them so well. Dorothy is at the wheel and Robert at the stern. Note the exterior speedo.

215 miles regularly up to Norfolk and back, then weekly 200 miles to Ashfield-cum-Thorpe where an old cottage was being converted. Bob's wife Dorothy now 86 years old, remembers well this their courting car, and the trouble free 500 miles honeymoon trip to Devon. Six years later a baroness who wanted an open car bought the 'R J' when young Vivien was on the way.

Bob and Dorothy Jones built a road haulage business which they both ran. In 1942 when Bob was drafted into essential war work, at A K Cooper of Sweffling, he maintained their fleet of dozers and winches engaged in clearing the massive airfields for the Americans.

Ironically, later on, Jack Jones (as they called him at Coopers) would often rush off donning his 'other hat' of Special Constable. His training in dealing with mass emergency would take him to nearby Parham, Debach and Horham where shot up Liberators and Flying Fortresses would crashland with horrific regularity.

The brain that master minded the 'R J' came up with many innovations. A twenty ton Low Loader, with knock out axles, and a central well in the floor to carry a Cat D6 blade, was a superb trailer indeed.

However Jack is remembered most for his redesign of the A E C Matador. As the Unipowers were phased out Jack converted about ten standard Matadors. Shortening the chassis by 2 ft 6 ins and fitting a superior Unipower winch inverted to line up with the drive shaft. With the new look cab this made an excellent timber tractor some of which are still at work today. Undoubtedly this man was a brilliant inventor and engineer.

A.K. Cooper's first Latil. To hold the Latil on course with the left hald, and wind up the brake wheel with the right, was an accomplishment only acquired by a few.

A scene in A.K. Coopers yard 1950s-60s.

This has to be the great cedar hauled by Coopers from Suffolk to the Royal Show at Blackpool in 1953. Rolling up big trees like this called for a skilled mate with cool nerves and clear hand signals and a driver with instant reaction to them.

Some of these conversions are still at work, and were liked by all the crews.

One of the ten smart Matadors. Jack Jones shortened and rebuilt with a Unipower winch.

The Williams Family

The Williams brothers George, Charles and Bert had a timber and general haulage business in Pandy Powys. With the demise of horse haulage they turned exclusively to Sentinel Steamers, winch tractors, two DG4's and a DG6 which made up an active fleet. George Williams retired in 1964 and sons Wyndham and Derek ran the firm for sixteen years.

Today Williams Timber of Norton near Bromyard is headed by George's son Wyndham, and his wife Molly. I imagined the Volvo haulage unit would be driven by their son Tony, but he has done his stint of log carting and found a new niche for talent in their tidy but busy yard dominated by several Bray loaders, from a faithful old 13 year old to current models. Tony designs and fits his own quick release change over systems for timber, grapples and forks. An expanded idea now accepted by several makers. His modern workshops offer a unique service. Experience has led Wyndham to become very Bray minded indeed.

But my eyes were already on a handsome beast — an Ex WD Thornycroft Nubian 6 × 6. Wyndham had replaced the Rolls Royce straight eight with an AEC 470 engine, fitted a jib, winch and anchor amidships. This fantastic timberman's "Go Getter" was enjoying a rare day or two at rest.

During the last war, aged only 16 years, Wyndham was sent on a most daunting mission. A local farmer had purchased a Cat D2 and Plough in far off Peterborough. Leaving at 6.00 am astride a Fordson industrial tractor with front mounted (Auto mower) winch and two trailers in tow. The farmer was huddled amongst the estimated cans of TVO for the 180 mile round trip, as they bounced along at 18 m.p.h., flat out. On arrival they learned the deal was off so turning round they romped the marathon journey through air-raids, getting home after midnight! One imagines the word "Fordson" stamped on Wyndham's backside! At 17 years, he was driving a Ministry Austin Artic Eagle Pole Wagon from Hereford into Hickmans of Wolverhampton. However, two early post-war favourites were Ex WD Chevs; one a Quad, that once hauled 600 cube of softwood; and a Chev Artic he ran 3 days a week to Leicester with 400 cube a time. On fitting Perkins P6, 500 cube became the norm.

As changes in the timber trade called for multiple butt lengths, rigid bolster wagons appeared, but try as he might, Wyndham could find no artic version. As far back as 1959, he saw potential in a surplus Atkinson rigid 8-wheeler. A fifth wheel coupling replaced the front 4 wheels, cab and engine. Wyndham then repositioned the 2 rear axles, and fitted bolsters and pins, thus producing the very first skeletal trailer, at least in those parts. This novel out-fit created great interest, but one critic predicted it would twist. However, it did not and similar trailers were soon being made by his firm. Well they do say imitation is the sincerest form of flattery!

Two years National Service as an aircraft engine fitter in the RAF gave Wyndham an excellent engineering background. He loves flying and has logged many hours piloting Austers for a hobby.

However, I have a feeling that above the clouds is not the only flying Wyndham did. In the old days, one regular job was running timber right up to Doncaster with

(Continued on page 33)

A Williams horse team somewhere in Herefordshire.

A close up of the sentinel steam tractor. Nothing is known of these excellent sentinel photographs, but each picture tells its own story.

The size of this tree is remarkable. Note the lumps of cordwood on each bolster to check the tree.

(Continued from page 29)

a Bedford QL. Having replaced the standard gear-box with one of his beloved Chevs, he reckoned she would almost take-off, often leaving others standing!

Servant bells still adorn the kitchen of the large Victorian house which is the home of this vibrant family of entrepreneurs who serve so well our timber trade today.

Just look at the size of that hefty winch!

Ready for the road.

One of the sentinel DG4s.

A Fordson industrial tractor with front mounted auto winch similar to the one Wyndham drove to Peterborough.

Wyndham once had 600 cube of softwood behind this favourite ex-WD Chev. Quad circa 1948.

To start with Wyndham never put more than 400 cube behind this 3 ton petrol ex-WD Chev. On fitting a P6 500 cube became the norm like these long ash he hauled to Leicester.

This ex-WD Commer 4 × 4 proved a valuable asset.

Wyndham's first jib. Counter balanced with plenty of chains.

Wyndham and Tony with the new 1965 Leyland Comet and Skeletal frame trailer they built from an Atkinson 8 Legger.

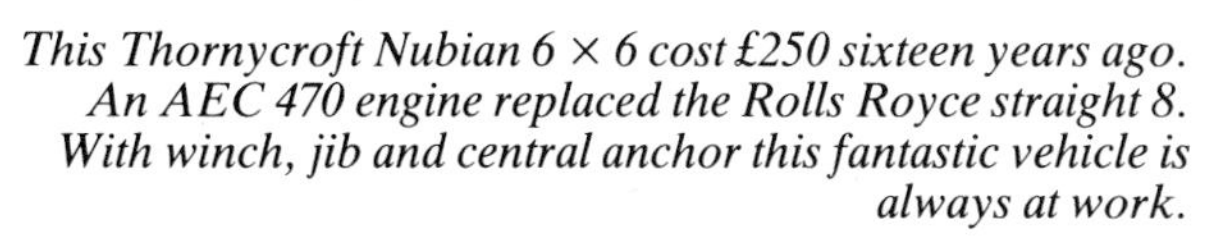

This Thornycroft Nubian 6 × 6 cost £250 sixteen years ago. An AEC 470 engine replaced the Rolls Royce straight 8. With winch, jib and central anchor this fantastic vehicle is always at work.

The Duggans of Pontrilas

In 1920 Maurice Duggan's father took a timber hauling job with Robert Wynn of Newport, Mon. The first morning Bob Wynn enquired what he had in the bag, and on hearing it was his dinner Bob said, "You'll not need that, you only get one meal a day here and that's at home before you start". There was to be nothing easy for the Duggans in timber. Maurice Duggan of Pontrilas handles his Matador and Volvo 8 wheeler as good as most, and better than some, 'so what'? Its just that when only sixteen Maurice lost his right arm in a motor cycle accident. It took over two years to come to terms with his artificial one, which he learned to use, not in a shop or office but as a welder of heavy timber equipment. In a short time he was building pole wagons, then eventually he started hauling with his own vehicle.

As his mind adjusted, his other arm gained power until he could put a bolster pin in position one handed with apparent ease. His only driving aid is a detachable handle for a steering wheel spoke, like that of a fork-lift truck. The police at a Ministry check point endeavoured to book him when he was driving an old tipper. The outcome of this was he took and passed a special driving test that led to his class 1 H.G.V. licence. His Matador has a left hand control disc winch brake but he

Driver Albert Duggan suffered crushing injuries destined to plague him the rest of his life in this Wynn Sentinel accident.

Albert lived in this van for weeks on end, all over Wales.

engages the right hand levers by reaching across, uncomfortably, with the left hand. His sense of humour is seen when a driver, unaware of his disability asked, "Can you give me a hand tomorrow?" Next morning this man found Maurice had left his artificial arm in his cab.

At twenty one Maurice's son Spencer prepares to take over the Volvo. A specialist tells Maurice his left elbow, that has doubled for the two so long, is now worn out and unlike hips and knees they are not into elbow replacements.

His using of chain saw and a Cat 995 are just astonishing. Asked how he has achieved so much Maurice says it is a matter of diverting aggression into the right channels. But to engage a Matador's right hand levers with the left hand takes some doing. There is a lot more to this man's abilities than he admits. Single handed he has earned his place in this book.

For some hills Albert had to change the sprockets as well as the gears on this chain drive petrol engined Scammel.

The Chair Leg! A poor snapshot but a magnificent episode. This is the Leyland Beaver Maurice drove all over the country. There is 780 cube in this elm. Maurice spent three days and broke two Matador winches trying to load it. Then Albert came and did the job in ten minutes flat. When questioned in a pub where they called, Albert, with pride, answered, "What that, that's only a chair leg!".

The Duggan Dance – Maurice lays his JCB loader over.

Archie and Bill Dodd

Archie Dodd's father and four brothers all worked for B and J Davies (Timber) of Bucknell. When Archie was a small boy, his mother despairing of her child's safety, tethered him on a long light chain around his waist to stop his wandering off with the horse teams. Even so, at 13 years, he could and did drive a steam tractor, at times on the quiet.

Between 1939-46, first in the RAF and then in Combined Operations Commandos, Archie volunteered for raids with the American Fifth, and British Eighth armies in places like Salerno and Anzio.

Eleven loads of timber waited at Bucknell one Friday. Archie, now demobbed and restless, heard the remark from Bernard Davies "Our name should be on those

One of the 6 × 4 Fodens Archie tested. Seen here with half of a 1,000 cube silver spruce at Wallcot Park, Bishops Castle. Archie covered 26,000 miles in six months hauling 6 to 700 cube on the first similar Foden. Courtesy Bernard Dodd

wagons." An idea that led to the purchase of an Ex WD 6 × 4 Foden chassis from Birds of Stratford. Archie tied a box on for a seat and drove her home, on trade plates. Davies built a pole trailer, made up from a Scammell tandem unit refitted with turned beam axles making up the back end. The Foden brought the first test load to the Railway Station Weigh Bridge with ease, but the ticket stamp revealed her load was 35 tons, and one trailer axle was bent. However, with redesigned axles, during 6 months Archie covered 26,000 miles, with 6-700 cube of timber on, from Builth Wells to London or Princes Risborough 3 times a week. The result of this trial was the purchase of 9 similar Fodens. One was built into a tractor and fitted with a Scammell winch; three more were made into artic units; two became flat bolster wagons and three were left as spares.

When Captain Dudley Simmons left the Royal Engineers and had recovered from being driven like the 'Clappers' by yours truly, he eventually joined the Vickers Armstong establishment at Chertsey. The Rolls Royce engined VR 180 Vigor was about to take shape and he became a development engineer.

The articulated track system allowing one to drive over logs at speed was not his brain child but the superb timber winch was his idea. The prototype tractor was tested at Camberley and on Bedfordshire clay. When Onion Bros linked up with Vickers in 1952, work transferred to the main works at Elswick, Newcastle on Tyne, where it was built.

Jack Olding Ltd., launched and acclaimed the Vigor as a world beater. No other crawler rode so smoothly, permitted gear change on the move and could reverse at 8 mph.

Forty Vigors helped build our motorways. The joint names of Vickers and Rolls Royce accounted for high sales around the world but sadly the whole venture closed in 1959. When it comes to after sales service back up, 'Caterpillar' run rings round all their rivals.

In the early 1950's Vickers, jointly with Onions Brothers, were seeking a site to test the new VR 180 Crawler and super giant logging arch. B and J Davies had just the job! At Downton Castle, 80,000 cube of timber lay on a most inaccessible hill. Every single cube was tushed down a near verticle drop, into and across the river Teme. The operator was Archie's brother Bill, who was already burning the soles of his boots off with a Cat D7 on this job. The incline was so steep no Vickers or Onions man, nor Bill's own mate, would ride up or down it. On every descent, the VR 180 would submerge her nose plunging into the river, drenching Bill with spray as he brought down butts up to 400 cube a time. Working from 5.00 am to 9.00 pm, both units came out well in this year of murderous timber extraction abuse. Bill was very impressed but declined an offer to demonstrate the machines across the world.

Archie recalls one of our dying breed, an old tree-feller, who's transport was a pony and trap, limping into a living van. His axe had glanced off a knot causing a deep flesh wound above the knee. Stemming the bleeding with one hand, he calmly asked for the needle and thread kept for garment repairs. Then, un-aided, he sewed up the gaping wound, winding a towel around it. Returning to his axe, he worked on until nightfall. By now, his leg was so stiff he could no longer stand, so two lads carried him and laid him in the trap and headed the pony for home. But resilient old "Snort" as they called him, was soon back. The calibre of this man was common at that time.

Archie's and wife Jeanette's home at Quatford nestles against sandstone cliffs. Monks could have enjoyed the vista of rolling Shropshire fields from this gorgeous

This hasty unloading shows us the Scammell Tandem drives. Courtesy Bernard Dodd

Archie hauled this 540 cube oak to Barchards of Hull, for trawler marking. Courtesy Bernard Dodd

A 706 cube Wych elm in a Derby Park. Quite the biggest tree I've seen loaded with sheerlegs. A Leyland Beaver and Unipower lifted it. Circa 1953.

Gently does it. This is a Foden 2 stroke tractor unit. At 25 tons surely this is an incredible weight for sheerlegs.

Loaded and ready to roll!

The first Vickers 180 makes her debut at Elswick works, Newcastle-upon-Tyne in 1949. Dudley Simmons is third from the left.

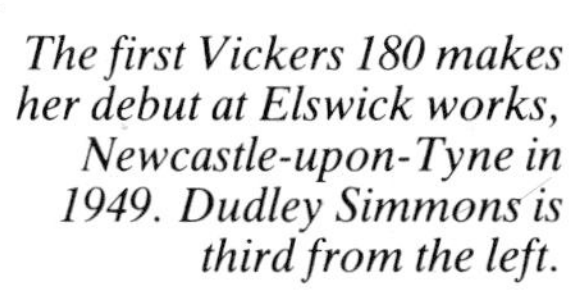

The Vickers 180 was worked a sixteen hour day throughout her tests with the Onions Sulky, which often overturned in the extreme conditions.
Courtesy Bernard Dodd

old house mentioned in the Doomsday Book. All long before puffs of smoke from the Severn Valley Railway which perfected this picture for me. A folly stands on the hilltop nearby, but Archie Dodd is nobody's fool! In both war and peace he has sought challenge and excitement, and found it both at home and abroad.

Archie, now retired, spends his days measuring and valuing timber for his brother Bill's son Bernard, and also enjoys a day's shooting and following the local hunt.

Bill Dodd, far right, stops for a moment to pose with the fallers. Courtesy Bernard Dodd.

Shirley Dodd at Hereford. Tushing out with a Caterpillar D7. This photograph featured on the Caterpillar calendar sent all over the world in 1951. Courtesy Bernard Dodd.

Ruth Kitching

If you were invited to chose a "Timber Loader" from a line-up of possible ladies, I doubt you would opt for petite Ruth Kitching of Stratford-Upon-Avon. Good looks and a slender build are no qualifications for tree work. Ruth met husband Harvey around 1951, and they both worked for a livestock transport firm. Fresh from the Coldstream Guards, Harvey made a few extra bob on Saturdays helping an old character Len (Juggins) Passmore, the stump blower at Hampton Lucy. Part-time fire wooding with an old tractor and bench, led to full-time mining timber, and later production of Pig Arks.

Harvey's first vehicle was a rough ex W.D. Chev. winch, which he used for everything, even his courting. The rare occasions they went to the pictures it was in the Chev! of course. It was 10 years before they married, due to lack of funds, but Ruth featured in it all right from the start. Harvey expected and found Ruth right beside him every step of the way. If it was felling, it was Ruth on the other end of the Cross-cut. The dreaded Danarm DD 8F Chainsaw with a kick like a mule was heaven after that. Delivering logs late every Christmas Eve took the joy out of many a Yuletide, the heavy sacks eventually injuring Ruth's back, during the winter times. Hot summers, brought longer hours of agony, and raw blistered hands from "bark peeling" for tanning, as day after day she slogged to realise the "Kitching dream!" The post war timber boom resulted in a yard, small mill and haulage. Ruth became loader mate on the Douglas timber tractor and 15 ton trailer, which Harvey purchased from Metcalfes of Leamington Spa. Lifting up the draw-bar to couple up was too much for Ruth. If no spare help was around, they would reverse roles, and Ruth would back the tractor up at the tick over, since it took both her tiny feet on the clutch pedal to effect this.

On the trailer ratchet brake Ruth excelled, and was quick to sense the push and pitch down the hills. Many of the long hauls required a 3.30 am start, returning around midnight. Pressing ever on, Harvey would never stop to eat, ascending long hills in "low cog", when Ruth would feed and pass him drink.

"Tushing out" with an old Marshall Pom Pom crawler Ruth did her own chaining up. The hairy rope, and falls in nettles were regular hazards she learned to avoid. A Fowlers International TD14 and a big Cat came later, as did a Unipower, that Harvey felt was well within her dextrous if dainty hands. In due course there were 40 on the payroll. Articulated pole wagons included a Guy "big J", Atkinson, three A.E.C.'s the ex Jabez Barker 6 × 4 Mammoth Major, and a Volvo FE88 6 × 4. Heading the fleet was the ex Turriff Construction MK 7-6 × 4 Foden 2-stroke registration number MNX 191E. She had reduction hubs, a 12 speed gear box and grossed at 75 tons with a big King low-loader. Loading was via three A.E.C. Matadors, one "Flat topped" ex RAF, one 6 wheeler, and one standard. Various flats trucks were included on the 10 vehicle operators licence. Administering this, invoicing, buying stores and fuel, hours, wages, you name it, Ruth did it, and raising three children as well. It is a mini miracle in itself.

On a Saturday morning, Harvey took one of the Matadors to his repairman Brian Calladine. The chassis was broken, the cab smashed and she was drinking a gallon and a half of engine oil a day. "Do what you like so long as we have it back for Wednesday", Harvey ordered. There was just one way to keep the deadline. Brian

Ruth with the ex-Metcalfe Douglas. Passing cyclists would help her as she struggled with coupling the hefty drawbar of the trailer.

cut off the front end and grafted in a K Reg Dodge tipper complete with its Perkins 6354 engine and gearbox. The beefed up front springs fitted the AEC axle, and with an air controlled winch and handbrake this old Matador became a real 'goer'. On test they got her up to 65 m.p.h. and the transplant proved most successful.

Harvey's pursuit of success took him all over Wales, Scotland and Cumbria buying timber. He lusted after a massive Elm on the Smith Ryland Estate, Barford, for over 15 years, before they were prepared to sell it. Likewise a press cutting tells how he similarly coveted two 90 year old Silver Spruces on Lord Dulverton's Estate, Moreton-in-the-Marsh. An electric storm in 1970 shattered the top of one of these Silver Spruces, and brought his wish ironically true. Due to the location of Warwick Castle, these big trees were carried out and loaded with a Matador holding each end. The operation had only one hitch, as the hefty stone one Matador ran over, turned out to be an old and valued tortoise. The Estate was most upset, as was the aged reptile.

Some comments in the Accident Book were humorously naive. In 1962 gems like — "Getting into the cab I damaged his car when he came too close!" — "The vehicle seemed to come in front of me from a side street!" who was to blame the weather? "Unknowingly I seemed to have damaged a parked car", no-one was to blame. "He over-took me, as I was over-taking" blame not stated etc, etc.

A precariously placed Street Lamp on the River Avon bridge was broken so many times by Kitching vehicles that the police always rang there first, enquiring, "Have any of your lorries gone over the bridge this morning?"

Then in 1980, just as it was starting to all be worthwhile, like a bolt from the blue came liquidation. All because they had failed to read some "small print" (the downfall of so many busy people). The Liquidators handy work devastated Ruth and Harvey, and this blow appeared to accelerate Harvey's failing health. Friends helped to restart the Saw-Mill, but it was too late. A knock from a falling tree years ago was behind his ailing back, later diagnosed as cancer of the bones. Then, as if in competition, heart disease the rival killer showed up in this "strapping" ex-Guardsman who died 3 years later aged 54. The blood sweat and tears of 30 years, all the energies Ruth had poured into the venture were now diverted to winding it up, only this time without Harvey's help.

Today, tending several Bonsai trees brings Ruth pleasure, and far less heart-break than their full size counterparts. A daughter and two sons of which she is proud, do her great credit. Three assets the Liquidators could not seize, from this tenacious lady.

Harvey with the ex-Jabel Barker AEC Mammoth Major. This lovely elm went to Furniture Industries, High Wycombe.

The popular Foden MK7 two stroke being loaded with the six wheeled Matador. This was a fantastic outfit. Her driver wore headphone ear protection as she roared across the Midlands and far beyond.

Ruth moves the Unipower between housework.

These 90 year old silver spruce at Warwick Castle were carried out and loaded by two Matadors. Then hauled to Mintos of Ponteland Co. Durham.

The 6 × 4 Volvo later sold to Mr. George Croasdale.

The Dodge cum Matador has a service. Note the Ford Ferguson nearby.

The Porlock Puller

Aileen and Bill Mattravers of Williton, Somerset rang to say they were now the proud owners of NYA 633 featured on page 46 in SORTH. This 1951 Forester made fame, after the Lynmouth floods, assisting a BRS eight wheeler Leyland Octopus on 1 in 4 Porlock Hill, with the sixty foot long girders for the new Lynmouth Bridge.

New and complete with low loader the Unipower came originally to transport "The Rat", a Priestman Wolf excavator, belonging to Edward R. Jones Ltd. Timber Merchant and Plant Hire Contractor of Minehead. Recovery became part of her regular duties. The vehicle was on full time emergency call to the police, being the only local winch capable of dealing with the habitual runaway spills on Porlock. The usual spot being on the bend where the gradient varies around 1 in 3 to 4. The simple if crude practice was to insert a girder into the chassis and put down a few straw bales to soften the return to even keel. By way of a change, when

A Type G Unipower and International Dozer. A crumpled but interesting photograph.

NYA 633 when new with trailer in 1951. What pride of ownership? Even the lowloader is beautifully signwritten.

the special Case L.A. Crawler used for towing Minehead Lifeboat stalled and became awash three hundred yards out at sea she dealt with this in her stride too.

Her days in timber ended early in the 1960's when Watchet Paper Mills purchased her for heavy haulage. Like so many of her contemporaries she was put out to grass with the advent of three line braking. In 1978 Bill Mattravers, who had often driven and always loved the old girl, just managed to beat the scrap man. Despite warnings from his firm "you'll never do it" the heap in the brambles became Bill's heap, under a sheet, which was to be the tractor's only cover throughout restoration, lasting three years. Much is written elsewhere of vehicle preservation, but in passing one must remember the difference from work carried out in the comfort of one's workshop with existing tools. NYA 633 was restored to perfection under the worst possible conditions. An unusual fact Bill and I have in common, is that we both have wives who hand painted our Unipower Foresters in green. But long before that Aileen, a trained geriatric nurse, got equally involved freeing rusted joints and getting this Pride of Porlock purring again. Since then they have worked it and rallied it from Cornwall to Brighton and the vehicle has become, not only their hobby, but part of their lives. Shovelling mud off the anchors, the odd C hook on the toes might have damped Aileen's enthusiasm had she worked this beast for a living but, 'fair dues' this is an immaculate restoration and serves well to remind us of the name Unipower, carved and kept in wood for thirty years or more.

Can you sense the excitement here? Recovering the model L.A. Case Crawler. Fitted with wooden bars on the tracks.

All over bar the drying out. Sea water makes engines very sick indeed.

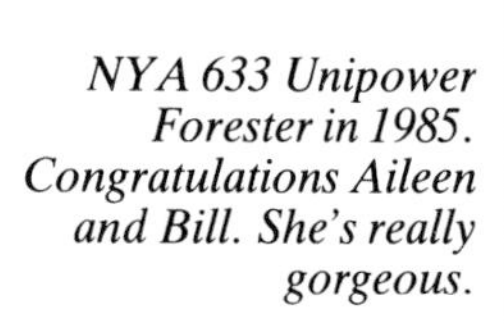

NYA 633 Unipower Forester in 1985. Congratulations Aileen and Bill. She's really gorgeous.

Maurice Weeks the transplanter

Readers of the TTJ may remember a regular advertisement by Maurice Weeks of East Harptree, nr. Bristol for ex WD vehicles he had adapted for timber work. An ex haulier, Maurice saw a gap for conversions, particularly for petrol engined vehicles to diesel. Starting with Perkins P6 he eventually replaced with Leyland, AEC and Gardners. A man, visiting his yard, once claimed to find no less than six tractors with engines other than which they had begun life. An Allis Chalmer HD7 with a Perkins, a Caterpillar re-engined with a Leyland and so on. Maurice's favourite ex WD vehicle was the FWD HAR 4×4 with an eight foot bonnet. One thousand two hundred of these right-hand drive artic. tractors were produced for Canada. Fitting a Garwood winch and anchor, he converted several of them.

His masterpiece was ex Chipperfield circus Mack 6×6 on which he mounted a specially big Auto Mower winch. The 1¼inch cable would lift and carry eight tons via the gantry Maurice designed. The line pull was never assessed. With ballast this 6 Lw engined 'Go-Getter' weighed about eighteen tons. When being called out to a forty ton Koehring 3 yard excavator, part submerged in sand, washed up by the sea, the crew of a 'Scammell Contractor' were parking up having stripped the teeth off their Darlington winch — and we have a ten speed drive they mocked. Maurice's son replied, "This winch drives through two gear boxes and has twenty five speeds". With the rope moving so slow, one could hardly see it move, this Weeks' built monster broke the suction instead of the winch, thus recovering the excavator completely.

This man's achievements were great; a most resourceful man of immense ingenuity.

Blemished, but important snapshots of Maurice with his FWD Model HAR. He fitted a new Meadows Diesel, 5 speed David Brown gearbox, PTO and Garwood Winch. Sold after 8 years Yeoman Service. HAR wheels gripped where others slipped, maintained Maurice.

The ex-Chippy. Mack 6 × 6 travels with a International BT Drott, with ease.

The Mack like Maurice rests on "Laurels Galore". This man's workshop was a veritable 'Papworth of the tractor world'. Engine transplanting was a gift and flair he developed.

Lucian the Lad who Loved Music and Wood

Any of you that have pondered the origins of "Furniture Industries", whilst waiting to unload at Latimer Sawmills, may be interested in the beginnings of this, one of our largest furniture makers.

Lucian R. Ercolani and his parents left their native Italy with help from the Salvation Army. The Social Headquarters of the S.A. in England found young Lucian a job in their joinery shop. It's no surprise that his musical talent found expression in their band. His father insisted, "Design is the basis of everything" and Lucian's gift to draw was already at work. Harry Parker, now Parker Knoll, introduced him to High Wycombe, and Ebeneezer Gomme did much to enrich his experience.

About 1920 the London Road works opened with a semi loco engine supplying the power. Growing steadily, their first Ministry contract in 1939 was for the humble tent peg, thirty six million of them. They took 400 cube of beech a day to make.

At the end of the war Mr. Ercolani was asked if he would care to buy the instruments from the disbanded Home Guard brass band. The idea of a works' band was exciting, although to employ the players was not anticipated, but worked out well in retrospect. This musical involvement brought many awards, and a sense of belonging, to all at Ercol.

In the 1950's I remember the long haul up to the mill and how sounds of a Sousa march, from the canteen, would gradually replace the drone of the loaded Foden.

Today something like seven hundred and fifty workers at Ercol, 'craft' the beauties of elm, ash or beech under the leadership of his sons, Lucian and Barry, far removed from the old Chiltern Chair Bodgers. "THE RULE OF THE WORLD IS SUCCESS; FAILURES ARE THE EXCEPTION". Words a little Italian lad learned in Shoreditch and proved in High Wycombe and around the world in his life in wood.

Prime timber being off loaded for Ercol's craftsmen to work. Wood that will live on and beautify someones home. Trees bound for Latimer sawmills have become a standard of comparison, such is the excellence set by this company whose slogan runs — 'Finished by hand — Started by nature'.

Sid Brightman had this favourite photograph framed. It depicts a Poplar, 510 cube and 50 feet long, loaded at Tiveton, Devon by a D4 and Jasper's Foden. Bound for Castle Headingham, Essex. This is my tribute to Sid who hauled from the West Country for 30 years and died in 1986. Courtesy Mr. John Boughton.

My Sussex Saunter

I bought my first Unipower from Bob Ansell of Wisborough Green in the 1960's. His congratulations on my book came with a reminder that Sussex had been overlooked, "Come down and see what you have missed" he said, and with this book in mind I did just that. Early, one gorgeous September morning, we set off literally down some of Bob's memory lanes. Every mile or so we would stop at some point of recollection and Bob would vividly relive an experience of his timber days. Just outside his birth place, East Dean, a battered old shepherd's hut is scarred to this day. Eleven year old Bob and pal Algy Lilywhite had rolled a big wheel down a hillock. The wheel crossed the road buckling the post master's bike and then the hut. During the war so many timber drugs used to park up on East Dean Green and often Jerry mistook the lot of them for gun carriages and strafed them.

Bob's first job was tea boy for the fallers. On accidently knocking a snared rabbit into the two gallon cauldron, the rabbit was smartly removed unseen, but the man who stirred a rabbit's eye in his mug was not amused.

On one side of a hedge, an overgrown heap of old Cat D4 track plates mark the spot of an overturned Latil. They were carried for weight ballast and could have killed old driver Bepton Bill as they fell around him. Bob drove his Range Rover up a Bridle-way where he had seen a German fighter shot down in the Battle of Britain. Some of it remains today, but the perspex cockpit cover was used for years, as a cloche by old Charlie Hoare.

We followed the trail of Speedy Davis the haulier, who had the first shaft drive Foden, and drove round in a big 12 cyl. Lincoln Zephyr. At one time Greens of Chichester employed over one hundred men at Singleton Sawmills, and they used to cut 2,000 to 3,000 cube of timber a day. Part of this Mill is still run by Algy Lilywhite, who favours the Muirhill Mobile Crane which was busy unloading. Nearby another rarity still works. A purpose built International Diesel B450/11 that can lift 7 tons and belongs to John Ruffell, a knowledgeable tractor man. Most exciting of all was yet another Crane, one of Green's two fifty-year-old steam Smiths of Rodley crane that still steams. Bob tells how its driver Henry Ward three times asked a tractor driver, who was winching a load off wheels astride the crane track, to move. The blunt refusal led Henry to push the tractor right to the end of the line.

I met Bob's old buddy Peter Croucher, who had for months driven Green's FWD the 125 mile trip. A job, down at Pendom Somerset, that was to last five years, and they were soon reminiscing about this and the great Devize's challenge. Here, thousands of cube lay on a steep hillside, when suddenly permission to extract from the bottom was withdrawn. Now how's this for ingenuity? A massive ex Admiralty Auto-Mower stationary winch whose 6 ft diameter drum housed over a quarter of a mile of 1¼ inch rope, and was powered by its own Fordson T.V.O. engine, was mounted on an F.W.D. This was fitted with 10ft long anchors made of Bailey Bridge sections. A Fordson tractor, that was used for pulling the rope down, was once winched up backwards with the 250 cube a time of trees, this fantastic winch could pull. It seems someone had waved the white flag before unhooking the tractor. A deserted crashed Air Force Glider lay in the woods, and, seen as better quarters, the lads all lived in it for months until one night it mysteriously got burned down. Peter Croucher once almost killed twenty cows at Manor Farm, Singleton, when his F.W.D.'s (with 500 cube up), brakes failed on the hill. Rushing along the narrow road into the farm yard he smashed through a gate whose post pulled out the end of the cowshed. Twenty of the cows, being milked, stampeded, choked and nearly hung themselves in fright and panic.

Passing through Chalton we paused a moment at The Fox Inn, famous for both the spoilt cooking of the landlady's Christmas cake, when Bob had brought down their power lines with an F.W.D. jib, and also the birth place of the Women's Institute. Although I saw or heard no trace of either Jam or Jerusalem.

The lunch Bob's wife had packed was enjoyed on the South Downs at glorious Goodwood. This was the scene of the great wartime timber overcut, and thousands of acres of prime Beech (many three for a load) were sold in what is believed national record timber sale transactions.

Harry Potter took on the disused West Dean railway station. Here, rotting in the undergrowth, was his famous old 'Bombay' export Unipower. Harry adapted it to drive a pneumatic teles chain saw. His involvement with ex W.D. vehicles ended with him buying Bedfords, eighty at a time, in Germany. Today, his two sons still specialize in ex Ministry and civilian rebuilds of this marque. Amid a sea of umpteen Bedfords on the scrub covered platform, Bob recalled the day that an harmonium had come in by rail. Station Master old Bill Musgrove, a keen organist gathered a crowd on the platform as he played hymns and songs. Some person distracted by the music left a 40 gallon drum of creosote on the line crossing. A passing train hit it and Bill was furious to find his house sprayed dark brown.

Didling Church snuggles beneath the Downs. This beautiful little shepherds' Church (only 46ft. long) goes back to the 13th century. The balusters of the altar rail are especially close to prevent attending sheep-dogs defiling the sanctuary. Outside stands the largest Yew tree I have ever seen and a smaller Yew. In the 1950's the church council wanted the small tree removing, and a faller offered to do this for the wood. By either accident or intent the old boy set into the big Yew, chopped back all the spurs and three parts axed the fall in before a parishioner spotted the error. This tough old Yew survived and the grown over axe work can be seen to this day.

The saunter finished as it started with a story of a wheel. We passed the spot where a 40×8 had come off Bob's trailer, bowled under some trees, hit the back of a Morris 1,000, rolled up and over it just clearing the ladies picnicking at the front.

Aged twelve, Bob loved to frequent Greens' workshop and landed a job there when he left school. When the yard crane could not cope with a glut of timber, Bob made and successfully fitted a jib to an F.W.D. round about 1947. Various hauliers envied it which led him to weld up one offs at nights and week-ends at a Stedham garage. With the proceeds from this Harry Potter took him to Ruddington where he bought a brand new Bedford QL for ninety five pounds, then a pole trailer for fifty pounds. When Bob's brother-in-law Maurice Handley left school he drove a CAT R2 for him, and later a P6 engined Commer Superpoise that was addicted to Aerostart. One job was so wet that slurry, not mud, on the road, went half way up a post box. Several fox hounds got so badly stuck they had to be rescued.

But manufacturing was to be Bob's niche. A purpose built sub frame, jib and anchor was designed. From 1960 a diesel Bedford RL was £650 and a Matador £850. Note this price was held for eight years. Up to five units a week went all over

CBP 58. The very first Foden STG 5 (hand start). Bunny Stevens drove her, a slope by his house ensured an easy morning start. When Fodens demonstrated a TG 5 Chain Drive Speedy Davis was not impressed. He told them, make a shaft drive and I'll have the first one, and he did.

the UK. Each tractor was new, taxed, painted and carried safety test certificates. Harry Potter bought the Matadors in Germany, and Bob and Maurice fetched them from Chichester railway station two at a time on a low loader. Long before plating and testing arrived, Bob foresaw the end of the 'home made' pole wagon. Approaching British Trailer Co. Manchester he became a distributor of the 32 ton pole trailer on 1400×20s and the 24 ton GVW single axle trailer on 1100×20s. Ordering forty for starters the business was most lucrative, but was short lived as the pole gave way to the skeletal trailer. Whilst others puzzled over '3 line braking' Bob courageously bought twenty thousand pounds of it and pioneered its fitting. Dozens of trade in Latils and Unipowers passed through his hands, some even twice. As a collector he once owned four hundred old farm tractors. His philosophy of life is summed up in his story of two shoe salesmen sent to Africa. One cabled back "Am returning, they don't wear shoes out here". The other urged "Send all our stocks, no one has any". Of his success and quality of life Bob made this simple observation. "I owe a lot to my wife. I couldn't have done all this without Rosemary". Sentiments many of us share but few get round to expressing.

Arriving at Midhurst, Bob's Range Rover was dwarfed by the stack of oaks when we drove into the old railway goods yard, which was the sawmill of W.L. West and Son. My interest was with Arthur West (known as Jim) who had from day one driven their Unipower TPO 899. This is the Forester that was later to serve me so well. It has now returned to its native Sussex.

Cecil West and his father Walter dug a sawpit on a plot outside the Half Moon Inn. By so doing they dug the foundations of a note worthy business headed today by nephews David and Robin West. Surviving and thriving they have now moved to a ultra modern mill out of town. Such is their faith in future forestry.

Jack Austin of Cocking is another of Bob's old school mates. As a lad he remembers four early Holt 30 caterpillars. Jack is another veteran of the great Goodwood beech cut. His life has been spent shifting timber with great skill, I've been told.

More men, mud and machines. A pack of fox hounds were stuck in the wake of slurry left behind by this Commer 'Superpoise'.

Day after day this Bedford QL and Bob churned away: Bringing the Commer and a sea of slurry out on to the road!

Bob with his next Bedford in drier times.

A corner of Bob's busy yard 1950s-60s.

Muir Hill had little success selling this Leyland 400 engined crane. But this one is well liked and soon removed this load.

John Ruffell's 1950 International crane is still at work and quite rare today.

Jack Austin roping out. I bet there were no Council roadmen about, I got reported for doing just this on the edge of the road.

No longer able to travel this Smith crane still steams in 1986. Her brilliant old driver Henry Ward sadly lost his nerve when a German machine gun bullet penetrated the roof in the Battle of Britain.

Greens favoured Unipowers. Jack had 400 cube in this beautiful oak veneer butt at Fernhurst.

First day out for this Hannibal at Compton, Sussex. Skid loading odds and sods takes time and temper, as many have found.

 Jack drove this Unipower OPO 136 from new in 1953 until 1970. Here seen with 500 cube of oak, bound for worthing sea defences.

Bob Ansell sold this shortened re-cabbed Matador to Greens. Jack welcomed the jib, here he is loading a 600 cube cedar at Goodwood Park.

Jim West poses having just driven home TPO 899, their new Unipower Forester in 1955. This family firm have survived the times and are still a most successful english timber company today.

Later this Unipower reversed roles, so to speak, and hauled hundreds of mature trees to our new cities. Here she loads a transplant on a special trailer for Gardner-Young of Tall Trees, Leighton Buzzard.

Jim West at Eaton Bray in 1985. Both man and machine have weathered well their days in timber. I purchased TPO 899 in 1978, my son-in-law Bill restored her. She has now returned to her native Sussex to work, my being no longer fit to handle her.

If in a hurry Have Hope

Fred Hope paid fifty pounds for a flat Ford lorry. His first job in 1944 was collecting Land Army girls from Rayners Lane Underground Station, at dawn, and taking them out to various farms in Middlesex. On a cold morning they would cram into a cab like sardines, and gear changing varied from embarrassing, difficult, to well-nigh impossible, yet not once did this red blooded nineteen year old complain. It was seen rather as a job perk to be enjoyed.

In the post war years Fred built a general haulage fleet and a name for reliable speedy service. The Hope vehicles carried the slogan that titles this story. Later, two double drive A.E.C. Mammoth Major Tractors came along for indivisible loads to be used for transporting 100 ft long 40 ton concrete beams mounted on a rear tandam axle bogey with an A.E.C. Mercury giving steering and added power. Two adapted baby alarms provided inter driver communication. The ensuing traffic snarl ups prompted a chief constable to write asking for the removal of the slogan boards for these units in the interests of driver frustration.

The success of this job led to a special assignment in 1962. R.C.A. (Radio Corp of America) on the behalf of the U.S. Government, required the transportation of 182 Oregon Pines, 105 feet long, from Liverpool to Thurso in Scotland. Fred's men worked out the route and got clearance from the hoards of affected authorities. These pines weighed about 5 tons each and were made up into 30 ton pay loads. They ran in convoys of six outfits, but with the lack of steerable dollies which were 10 feet wide, some units had to negotiate corners with a 40 foot overhang. R.C.A. insisted on discretion since this was a secret project. One imagines that with the police estimate of over 1,000 vehicles held up at one point alone, one or two motorists at least would question the cause. The media, national and local presses alike, featured the chaotic delays these long loads incurred. I've read press cuttings of town council rows and some town councils who tried to stop the convoys completely, but it seems once permission was given only an act of Parliament could do this. A party of lawyers travelling to Norway missed their boat due to delays and threatened to sue Hope Transport. In spite of police escort, when crossing a carriageway, Minis and sportscars would tend to duck under the slow moving loads. Never before had such loads travelled the Highlands. A double hairpin bend at Helmdale took eight hours to negotiate. Even so the local police inspector rang Fred and told him the drivers had done a marvellous job. The biggest sweat of all must have been in a little Scottish town centre, when one driver got well and truly jammed on a corner. With only a foot or two ahead of him and the tails almost touching the Town Hall doors there seemed no answer, then someone had the bright idea that opening the doors would give another foot or two. A reluctant town clerk eventually obliged, and the huge gold embellished double doors were opened revealing a large foyer. With great skill, driver Jock McVee inch by inch reversed foot after foot of the overhang right into the hallway which enabled him to complete the manoeuvre. When this most exacting and perilous job was done one of the drivers questioned: "Did not any similar trees grow in the U.K?" The answer came from one of the Americans: "Trees, these are not trees, they are tops of the trees we grow in the States."

Being on the road for eight days with the same load called for ingenuity even down to the crews doing their own washing and stringing it out along the load.

Fred sold his transport business in 1966 so that he could concentrate on his brain child the Hope Anti Jack-knife Device, a safety device now used the world over. Hope Technical Developments Ltd. Ascot, Berks, is headed by Fred Hope, the kind young lad who regularly suffered a cab full of Land Girls over forty years ago.

Just one of the cornering problems the crews faced continuously.

Imagine how hairy it became when sports cars and impatient mini drivers ducked under these loads crossing road junctions.

Both braking and gear changes were synchronized between the two tractors via an adapted baby alarm system.

Jock McVee had a 40 foot overhang and no steerable dolly when he reversed his load right into the Town Hall foyer. No wonder onlookers stood spell bound.

The Wood Waggoners

Seeking to cut back on the free copies of SORTH for review, I looked again at the Association of Professional Foresters. How many of these Arborists would relate to it, I wondered? Fortunately, as it happens, I gave them the benefit of my doubts. I had seen them as forestry academics brandishing their college diplomas in the woods, and up to 1960, to some extent, I would have been right.

A handful of men broke away from another society to form a more down to earth (or is it sawdust) association. Today men and women in every aspect of forestry share a unique facility in the APF. Members themselves organize a bi-annual working forestry machinery demonstration, now believed to be Europe's biggest. The timberman's every need, from a bowsaw blade to a £80,000 harvester, is shown at this spectacular three day event.

For me, my book brought a rave review; an invitation to speak at the conference; the opportunity to raise about £250 for the provident fund from sales; honory membership and a great wealth of new friends. All great benefits I've come to enjoy.

At Clumber Park APF 1986 I met Dereck Megginson of J. Taylor and Sons, Driffield, reminisced about four generations of wood waggoners out at Holme-on-Spalding Moor, near York. John Hall was seventeen and his sister just sixteen years old when they shared driving their father's Ford lorry. They drove daily from tea time to 2 a.m., this being about the hour their father would set off seventy miles to Hull. Later John's father had a 30 cwt. Ford which had a third dead axle and 15×5×6″ body. Four tons of round timber was the norm, and rearing up was off set with plenty of chains and loose gear in the cab, but steering was still dangerously light. Their sole customer was Kitching's of Knaresboro' who saw the problem of the short Ford. They financed a new Commer artic unit on the strength of a verbal agreement. There's trust for you! John's father never really mastered reversing an artic. First day out, six horses dragged the unit backwards off the road into the wood. After that they always reversed with young John turning the wheel, as he stood on the running board. This was a skill that earned him a few bob in wood yards from other drivers endeavouring to back their new fangled artics.

In due course the Commer succumbed to the Hall's loads when on a hill with a fair load of oak, John changed into bottom gear and the cab leapt up like a tilt cab. The chassis had broken clean both sides between the spring hangers, but undeterred, he chained and roped it down enough to reach the hill top farmyard. Such incidents filled this man's story.

Timber growing in a deep ravine was so inaccessible that the buyer flew over to price it. John remembers this because of extraction nightmares, and he was actually paid tuppence a cube extra without asking.

Endeavouring to keep the 'Open A' license on his father's retirement was an anguish typical of those days. Public opposition coming from transport firms not in timber haulage, and also the railway who could not deliver logs coming into the goods' yard, yet opposed John's application to do so.

Mr. Taylor, Timber Merchant, of Driffield, offered John a job to drive an ex WD Dodge. Later he took over their ERF from a driver who so lacked confidence that he would crash his gear change if looked at, so his mate had to look out of the window each time! For the same reason, all authorised passengers were made to ride outside in all weathers.

An interesting vehicle was a Foden 8 wheeler cut down and made into a 6×4 with 15×20 singles on the rear double drive. This was a real goer says John, as the engine and gear box were so good that given enough 'revs' on a hill he could lift the front wheels up off the road and keep them there until he eased back his foot. John drove this favourite wagon until 1965 when he slipped off a load and broke his back, consequently John's son Barry took over Taylor's various vehicles until they ceased their own haulage.

Today Barry Hall (round timber haulage) runs a DAF 2500 8 wheeler and Atlas loader. After an artic Barry prefers this wagon for getting about his jobs. With power to spare, he says an extended chassis and a third rear trailing axle would be ideal. Barry operates about a radius of 200 miles, with his youngest daughter Marie. Twenty year old Marie is counting the days to her twenty first birthday. Her ambition is the key of the DAF, not the door, i.e. to take her HGV test. As a child she loved going with dad and was smitten at an early age. She tells me, she decided one day, at about the age of twelve, that she would drive 'a wood wagon'. This was no idle aim, and on leaving school she had set her mind on this profession and has never had any desire to do otherwise. Accepting her determination Barry agreed to train her, and she learned to drive on their first DAF artic as soon as she could reach the pedals. She progressed from moving round the log piles to carrying out all off the road driving. With methodical care Barry taught her how to use a full size chain saw, without getting pinched in the cut, right through to strapping on the load. Handling the DAF in sawmills turns a few heads but Marie is a very determined lady.

By the time you read these words its safe to expect she will have that magic piece of paper. In this book of all our yesterdays in timber it is refreshing to feature Marie and the plans for her tomorrow. We welcome her to this rough, tough trade of ours where I know this latter day lumberjill will succeed.

The Hall story started with a young girl driving a lorry and history is set to repeat itself four generations later. Good luck Marie.

Barry Hall at the wheel of the cut down Foden 8 wheeler, in 1965. Putting the toe down on a hill could lift the front wheels off the road for yards! Such was the power of this motor.

Barry with the first load on Taylor's H Reg. Bedford.

Barry and Marie with their DAF in 1987.

Marie turns a few heads as she shunts the DAF at the sawmills. Welcome to our profession Marie.

APF 1986 where I met so many of you, including Ian Ferguson of Carlisle, who made this model chainsaw from Balsa Wood. His nerve enables him to climb both dangerous trees and be seen wearing this headgear, even in Tesco's, he tells me.

One of the well maintained older outfits operated by Mrs. Sheila Brunton of Eridge, Sussex, who died recently.

One old timer wondered just what this harvester did then concluded with "The old timber job was always hard and cruel. But with sheens (machines) like this, hard work was never easier".

Michael Oates of Worksop sends this wartime scene of their Foden.

The name Blackpool for me conjures up the tower, Dixon, the organ. Al Yates and Peter Wood, tree specialists, of that town had all the stops out on this old Major as she reared and rocked bringing a six ft. diam. tree up a bank. One imagines the stench of clutch burn that prevailed.

The Lakeland Loggers

Meandering up a Lake District pass whilst on holiday years ago I was overtaken by a six wheeled Leyland Riever loaded with pulp wood. Cumbrian Hauliers, Hawkshead, was the name remembered as the driver dropped a cog and passed. Barbara and Gilbert Brown, with sons Iain and Andrew, run a close knit fleet of eight specialist timber vehicles. Let Leyland critics beware; this make has dominated here for years. Gilbert claims it pays and is patriotic, and I think he has had enough to know. A ten year old 'Octopus' is running proof of great economic sense, and a further eight year old one is in absolutely immaculate condition. Pride best describes the cab liveries of orange and white. A beautiful painted Hawks head denotes their village and each wagon is named with the prefix 'Lakeland' followed by either:- Raider, Hunter, Tramper, Wanderer, Rambler, Forester, Roamer and Logger; all names chosen by their respective drivers.

Come sunshine or rain, which usually comes sideways up there as I recall, the Browns are responsible for delivering 350 tonnes of pulp wood a week from local Lakeland forests to the vast hungry Thames Board mill at Workington. Spruce sawlogs for conversion to building industry timbers are also collected for a subsidiary company within the Thames Board complex. Pulp wood and saw logs are also collected from special rail trucks at the nearby station. Small coaster ships also arrive at Workington docks, from the west coast of Scotland and the Scottish Isles, with similar timber which is discharged from the boat onto trailers supplied by Cumbrian Hauliers. It is fairly common for this firm to handle 1,000 tonnes of timber per week for Thames Board Ltd.

Many of the various trailers are also taken deep into the local forests for loading. For nine years this was done with a shunt unit and a hydraulic timber crane mounted on a four wheel drive Bedford RL. Neither Leyland nor any other firm in Europe could supply the vehicle Gilbert had in mind to replace this method of working. Eventually, a bonneted 4×4 V.10 air cooled Magirus Deutz was purchased second hand. It has a ten speed splitter gearbox, high and low range gearbox and cross axle diff locks. That's as imported. Hawkshead designers then took over and the truck was converted to an all wheel drive artic unit. The suspension had to be lowered and the chassis strengthened and it was then fitted with one of Atlas Cranes' biggest lorry loaders. Gilbert specified that it had to pick up a ton at 38 foot of reach to enable it to load the longest trailers. It had hydraulic extending outriggers with a spread of 22 feet. A sliding fifth wheel makes sure that the unit can accommodate all trailers.

Maggie's job is to take trailers off the road, load and return them. In some cases up to six miles into the forest, notably at Ennerdale. Trailer brakes are independent to the tractor to prevent jack-knifing when descending steep forest roads. The vehicle can easily load 20 tons of sawlogs in 20 minutes, and up to twelve trailers per day can be loaded if the unit has not far to move them. It is an ironical fact that the very first hydraulic timber loaders, brought into this country from Sweden, were demonstrated locally in 1967 by a young lad named Cyril Brayton. He has driven for Gilbert for many years. These original loaders were marketed under the name "FOCO" crane.

The Brown ingenuity goes back to Gilbert's Grandfather. A press cutting tells

Gilbert's grandfather loading timber near "The Drunken Duck Inn" in 1938. This Bedford later became an artic.

how he floated trees from the Lakeland Island with a 1¼ h.p. in board engined flimsy boat. His 1937 Bedford flat truck had its body removed during the war to become an artic pole wagon. The photograph in the 'Dalesman' has to be this Bedford seen near Kendal with additional h.p. Until two years ago, in spite of modern equipment, in the Lakeland valleys horses were still used to extract first thinnings. Gilbert describes how a trusty animal would, quite unaided, pull timber down the hillside around boulders and obstacles. If the traces were then undone the animal would return of its own accord.

Cumbrian Hauliers are a lively example of a hitherto dying breed dedicated to Leyland Trucks. 'Family Timber Hauliers' — long may they show the British flag around our English lakes and dales.

Four extra horse power for the Bedford at Kendal in 1940. Courtesy The Dalesman and Howard Nunnick.

Leyland line up. Sons Iain and Andrew and joined by Gilbert, in overalls, with 'Lakeland Rambler's' driver. The following photographs give some idea of modern woodland harvesting methods.

The imposing 4 × 4 Marigus Dutz 'Lakeland Forester' that takes the trailers six miles off the road into the forest. The driver is just replacing the thirty eight foot outreach crane.

'Lakeland Rambler' off loading softwood from the special rail trucks. Since 1967 Thames Board Ltd. has grown to become the most modern mill in Europe. Your cornflakes packet probably came from carton boards processed from a load like this.

'Lakeland Raider' backgrounded by Coniston Village and water. Scene of Malcolm Campbell's fatal water speed record attempt.

'Lakeland Tramper' sets off for Workington.

The Hexham Story

In 1942 four trucks of a train load of resin caught fire in Wolsingham, Durham goods yard. The prompt action of uncoupling and winching them clear by the crew of a timber tractor brought commendation from the Railway Company.

When Martin Jackson of nearby Bridge End Sawmills, Hexham, sent for a CORDA tape I asked him if he knew of this incident? This chance enquiry led to a most enlightening insight into both the climatic and geographic differences in northern timber operations. Southerners saw Arthur Green's 'Sheerlegs' as lunacy and it is no secret that skid-loading was loathed north of the Trent. Terminology differs as they 'lead' not 'haul' to a sawmill up north.

It was the mention of two Foden 8 wheelers still at work that did it. Just down at Slaley, Maurice Henderson and son John, beaver away at the family business they've built. NNL 746, an ex Blue Circle Cement Foden 2 stroke, is now retired. To hear her regularly come loaded up the 1 in 4 and 1 in 3½ Hadrian country hills must have been music indeed. Twenty seven year old YYR 429 ex Hovis Bulker brings the timber in daily whilst younger CRH 415 C delivers the sawn products. "In spite of age they talk through their tests", Maurice said with pride. All Maurice's three daughters have worked in the mill at various times. "Irene", he said, "used the Rackbench as good as any man before her marriage".

Of the horse days Maurice recalled a big Clydesdale that had gone down, and he raised it to its feet with a fork lift truck, proving one of two things. He must have either been one of the last to use horses or the first with fork lifts.

The Electricity Board wanted fifty thousand pounds to bring the mains to the mill, so a generator is driven by a Mirrless Blackstone engine. The price of diesel has led Maurice, (an ex threshing contractor) to permanently install his 43 year old Robey portable steam engine to take over, running on wood waste alone. "Is this some short term nostalgic gimmick?" I queried. Maurice looked stern and said "It's long term sense the way oil is going". The Henderson Mill may lack computers but it is efficient and profitable. Thanks in part to two aging Fodens and an ancient Robey.

Matthew Walker was a canny traction engine-man, which he had to be, as demonstrator for Clayton Shuttleworth of Lincoln. This led to becoming manager of all steam vehicles operated by Lanchester Council in County Durham until they were phased out in 1926. He then purchased a small coal business which had 3 lorries. Later he met Dryden Ward.

Dryden had removed the front axle and shafts of an old horse drawn timber wagon, and with help from the local blacksmith, the backend, pole and front bolsters were pinned to an old Model T Ford. It was only a small matter of time before the Smithy's shop rang with industry, as each of Matthew's coal lorries in turn, denuded of bodies, were given a pneumatic tyred articulated pole trailer.

By now Arthur Green of Silsden, Yorkshire, was buying timber all over the British Isles and wanted "go anywhere" hauliers to deliver into local railway yards. Matthew Walker, and 14 year old Matty took up the challenge. The business grew rapidly, and soon 6 horses, a Robey steam tractor, 3 Fowler 4/40 crawlers and Latil tushed out and loaded the growing fleet of artics of Dodge, Commer and International Marque. They were hauling for Claridges of Exeter, Snows of

Glastonbury and Stennings of Reading. But longer hauls and bigger loads were called for, so in 1934 with a lot of courage, nerve and money Matthew went to Fodens ordering a brand new tractor unit, and a custom-built tandem axled artic, pole trailer made to the Walker specification. In its day this outfit was seen as "timber haulage par excellence". Sensational was the description when she opened up her first big long term job, running from Ponteland (north of Newcastle Upon Tyne), right down to Woolwich Arsenal (South London). A lad called Ozzie Thompson drove her, and "she ran the elite" Matty said, with pride, then explained how a whole fleet of big Armstrong Saurers ran nightly down from Aberdeen to London carrying fish. These men and their vehicles really were something! Right up the great north road they were known as "The Elite". If you were able to keep up with these boys, with that class of wagon, then you too could claim to "run with the elite". Chief qualifications being: getting done regularly for speeding, overloading and hours at the wheel. Ozzie's membership was assured since he averaged 600 cube of green Beech a trip down to the smoke, no mean achievement in the late 1930s. At the Cinderby Café with its' welcome hot stove and full-length "Kip Couches" the Foden was nicknamed the "Silent Ghost". The A1 had miles of invitations to coast, especially between Catterick and Boroughbridge. By day and night Ozzie would "free the cogs" and reckoned to roll around 55 to 60 mph for miles. Long before he appeared one could hear the wum! wum! wum! characteristic sound of a big load trailer as she coasted, in otherwise silence, like a ghost of the road. The phantom Foden became a legend of the North, and West country also. After service in the Royal Engineers Matty became an Earthmoving Contractor, but sadly his father was lost in the Plymouth blitz.

Sadly I had to decline Martin Jacksons invitation to visit and see first hand the rigours of extracting rich harvests of northern forests. Kindly, Martin sent Hexham to me, via a cine film and tape; he's that sort of fellow. In Sherwood's Glade at the A.P.F. was an obvious place to meet Maurice and Martin, and friends Eddie Tulip and Arnold Halliday.

Eddie's mother worked in a sawmill and he knew a father and daughter regular felling team. Of his memories I remember most of the following. He was working near Alnwick the day a 9lb axe glanced and took every toe off one faller's foot. How he once rescued a drowning horse that had slipped into a deep narrow stream. Trapped on its back, the water rose to cover its head. Gently with a cat D6, Eddie pulled it out, quite unharmed.

Young Arnold Halliday's first job in timber was to be sent up to the shop for a tin of treacle to put on a slipping belt. Dipping his sticky fingers in the tin got him a clip round the ears. To qualify for a faller they were required to split a match with an axe swung both over the left and right shoulder. In the woods any youngster becoming stroppy, would, when up a tree to fasten a cable, find the ladder removed. The fallers would saw away with glee, replacing the ladder just before the tree fell. When talking about sawing at ground level, Arnold, who now owns his own mill, was most emphatic about low cutting. Six inches at the bottom is worth six feet at the top he assured me, on ending our brief meeting.

From Kielder across the Cheviots, Wark, down to Slaley, Northumberland's timber challenges man and machine beyond the point of endurance. For half an hour the film took me round the modern mill, Martin and son Michael run. Out at Whitfield they faced getting 85,000 cube over the West Allen River without a bridge. I looked on as fallers, drivers and these two men built a bridge 130 yards long out of about 950 cube of timber. No flood moved this well cabled construction. I saw Martin's S reg. Bedford and 4in line pole trailer cross over with about 600 cube up. The camera followed her turning onto a steep hairpin bend that has to be Whitfield's answer to Porlock. Elsewhere Martin's logging arch, a converted Bren Gun Carrier linked to a TD 9, led trees over a peat bog. From a hill too steep for tractor or horse the Jacksons big County tractor and tower " Skylined" trees up to 50 cube for five hundred yards on a double overhead rope-way, Norwegian style. All this and more culminated at an axe and sawing contest.

Responsibility came early to Martin, aged 18, when his father was seriously injured in a timber accident at a Travelling Sawmill. Best of all Martin and a friend, Harry Shirewell, gathered some of the old brigade at the Pack Horse Inn, Stanhope, Wear Valley. Old times were relived, and photos swopped. Jack Grey, and timber merchant and farmer Frank Ward, Frank's wife Audrey and others all shared a few jars over a tape recorder. The wealth of memories mostly concerned Frank's father, Henry Dryden Ward, a name legend in the north. Running from Aberdeen to Woolsingham with Foden Artics was about a fifteen hour run legally. The time could be halved by returning a different route to foil the police, who would time and wait for them. Weigh bridges recorded up to five tons overloads and five blow outs on one trip confirmed it. This impossible site required a crawler to pull them in and two to drag them out loaded. On the road the units were so out of line the driver would bump the kerb with the back end to straighten up. One driver that did not, came all the way home with the near side trailer wheels beside the kerb and the Foden running just over the white line. The name of the game was initiative, sweat and keep the wagons rolling.

Dryden Ward started with one horse in 1912, eventually progressing to fifty. An

Reg. NNL 746. This ex-Blue Circle Cement Foden 2 stroke 8 wheeler gave Maurice Henderson exceptional service.

Reg. YYR 429. Ex-Hovis Bulker Foden 8 wheeler. John Henderson brings timber in from a wide area on this 27 year old Foden.

Reg. CRH 415C Foden 8 wheeler delivers sawn timber right down the country. Like her older sister she walks through her test every time.

early set back came when he lost four horses over a cliff top. Without funds to replace them, a friend loaned and worked his own horses for Dryden. Later, when hard times hit this friend and he was outbid for a Clydesdale at a sale, Dryden heard, bought and delivered the horse to him, thus repaying the favour. He showed his horses and won prizes. He loved them, and finally one took him to rest in 1960.

Expanding, he bought standing timber for his fifteen sawmills. Hauling first with traction engines and steam Fodens, he later had Fords, and then from 1936 six wheeled Foden diesels came. Fodens made Dryden a valued customer, although the red neckerchief he wore had them guessing, on his first visit, when ordering the first of his fifteen wagons. His biggest achievement had to be in 1950, with a ten year job on an island in Loch Tay. He gave £1,000 for an ex-naval landing craft that ferried the trees over at 1000 cube a time. The landing craft, sixty feet long, fifteen feet high and wide was low loaded by one of the Fodens from Dunbarton, twanging telephone wires all the way. Business acumen, tenacity and vision, all qualities combined in one name . . . "IT'S H. D. WARD LTD" . . . as painted on the cabs of his beloved Fodens.

Nine pound axes, landing craft, skylines, YES, there is a north south divide, at least in timber, and Martin Jackson has shown us it.

The 43 year old Robey engine that runs on wood waste and saves £50,000 plus.

Wee Matt, aged twelve, marked with an X. An Aunt sent this post card of the two Commer coal lorries the village blacksmith converted to artics.

Matty now sixteen years plus pulls the Foden out with their Fowler 4/40 under the watchful eye of a gamekeeper.

More of the Foden 'Silent Ghost'. Just look at the bolster pin!, the chains that hold the top trees, then think of Ozzie rolling along at 55 to 60 mph out of cog.

Another 600 cube load in the west country for Snows, Claridges, perhaps Stennings. It was pre-war, money was tight, days were long and timber was booming.

Whitby Chapele Hexham 1930. Martin Jackson's father had several mobile sawmills set up in the woods, powered with engines like this steaming on wood waste. Thousands of wood blocks for Newcastle streets were produced from mills like these.

There was about 500 cube of silver spruce on this ex-WD 3 ton Chev. Artic: How did they take those hills?

Martin's Turner diesel tractor, a great favourite of his, nowadays a most rare animal indeed.

Martin's yard today. The Leyland swings in with some fine oak butts, followed by his Bedford and 4 in line trailer.

Eddie Tulip sent this nice snap of a standard Fordson and Hendon winch.

How to transport a crawler on a bolster wagon; who needs ramps to unload? Eddie in Argyll in 1950.

Eddie felled a whole stand of these larch, 60 feet long plus, and not a branch on them. They were lead down by R. Minto and Sons of Ponteland.

Five of the fifty horses that worked the Northumberland Forests for Dryden Ward.

87 *Dryden's first artic, an AEC with a formidable load.*

This is a 24 HP 30 CWT Ford with a very extended pole. A second print shows about a 10 feet overhang!

What a delightful picture.

89 *The day of the Fowler and axe.*

Two tractors would pull the Fodens off a disastrously wet job in Aberdeen. This would distort the units so much, the drivers would bump the rear wheels on the kerb to realign the outfits.

Not much room for the big one on top.

The landing craft that carried a 1,000 cube a time across Lock Tay for 10 years. Circa 1950.

A scruffy snap, but a fantastic scene. found in the Foden toolbox perhaps?

The fleet line up. Foden's looked upon Dryden with caution when he arrived at Sandbach wearing a red neckerchief to order the first of fifteen Fodens.

Its H.D. Ward Ltd.

Frank Ward today. Still faithful to Foden.

Arthur Green Remembered

Many ex-Arthur Green men made themselves known to me at the APF Clumber Park. One of them was Des Pickard of Skipton, Yorks. A retired Caterpillar driver. He brought a box full of photographs and I picked just twelve of these gems for your pleasure. Thank you Des. They are superb.

ARTHUR GREEN

PNG 501F

Three Snapshots from Grange over sands

More APF delights - Dad's old Leyland Wagons! A proud caption from a family album. 'Dad' Donald Tuer drove both these Leylands for Barkers.

Donald Tuer (centre) sent this unusual model ERF for us.

Barker's old Leyland Badger with a fair load.

Jimmy the Winch

Sadly I declined the invitation to organize stressful timber loading demonstrations at Motor 100, Silverstone, 1985. Clive Peerless and Geoffrey Evans of H.C.V.C. persisted. If collected would I attend committees, acting in a purely advisory capacity. Five months on I was still doing just that as I joyfully drove my Latil round the track, leading a Matador, Foden and Unipower.

My old friend Brian Freer of Stoke Albany, Leics., came up with his Scammell and King low loader carrying his pole wagon and Unipower Hannibal, named 'Pogles Wood' by his children. Brian's 14 year old son Ben handled 'P.W.' with dexterity. At one time there was a programme for children on the television called Pogles Wood about a puppet family who lived in a forest and also had a lorry, hence the name. Ex-guardsman Brian has long since left timber. Keeping a Fordson magneto overnight in the oven, etc., is part of his enterprising past. Today the Freer's low load contractors plant on and off the motorway repair sections.

The most noteworthy accomplishments are those of the oldest son Jim, who was born two months premature, weighing less than four pounds and with cerebal palsy in lower legs. He learned to walk by the age of five, and many years of corrective operations on the achilles tendons of both legs have resulted in some measure of success. To eventually drive a tractor in the field was a great achievement. Passing his driving test the first time in a conventional car soon after his 17th birthday, again was really something, but to consider H.G.V. had to be a pretty wild dream. Yet at twenty one this tenacious young man took and passed his H.G.V. class 1 on a Scammell and low loader. He regularly drives both their own Crusader, and a local Volvo F10 6×2. Recovery work with the Unipower has earned him the name of 'Jimmy the Winch'.'Pogles Wood' once recovered a CAT D9, bellied with a blade and ripper, via a 4 to 1 rope reduction, with a CAT D6 and a 955 hooked on as anchors. The day before we talked, a loaded tri axle grain bulker was bogged down in a harvest field; axles, landing legs, the lot. The aroma of Volvo clutch

Timber loading line-up at Motor 100 Silverston 1985. Left to Right – Ben Hinton, Bernard Berrows, Jim Hutchins self, Brian, Ben and Jim Freer and Allen Lawrence. What fun we had!

'Pogles Wood' Brian Freer's Unipower Hannibal Series 12, new to Walkers of Syston, Leics. Jim had clay up to 'Pogles' toolboxes pulling out this 46 ton of Volvo and grain.

Jim checks the load, prior to his journey with the Scammell Crusader.

linings still pervaded the air when Jim arrived with 'Pogles'. The flimsy F10's front draw bar objected to "P.W.'s" assistance, so careful placing of slings from the rear had poor old 'Pogles Wood' wound back down to her tool boxes in clay, although a Fergy 2640 was holding her down as well. Finally free, the farm weighbridge recorded 46 tons plus, to everyone's astonishment.

Jim has had some long hauls and there are more to come, but none will be so long as the haul to get that 'class 1'. Who else could have worked so hard to earn it?

George Randall's daughter has fond memories of school holidays spent on these Foden steamers. The makers sales material featured this photograph with the name Foden displayed in lieu of Coltmans.

The Two Georges

Coltman Bros. Ltd. of Claybrook Magna, Leics. were most respected members of our trade. Two stalwarts of the haulage were George Randall now deceased, and George Whiston who now suffers failing health and could not be interviewed. These photographs loaned by his wife are a tribute to the firm, and the splendid men who served well their day and age of horse, steam and oil.

One of Coltman's two Foden TG 5 chain drive tractors and Foden build timber carriage. In a letter to Fodens, dated 25.4.35, the brothers wrote – 'our first tractor averages 66 miles a day per 6 day week. Consumption of crude oil was 38 galls, therefore running costs including grease was not more than £1 per week. The tractor pulls a 6 wheeled carriage with loads as big as the law allows'.

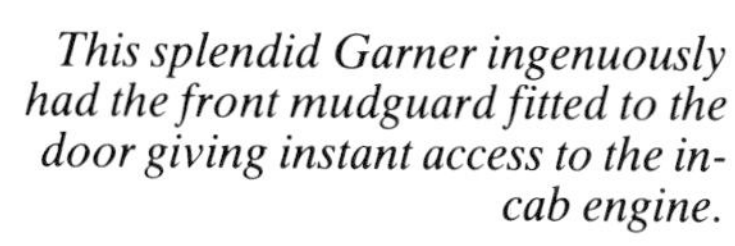

This splendid Garner ingenuously had the front mudguard fitted to the door giving instant access to the in-cab engine.

Top cart with the 5 ton Foden.

Skid loading at its best, all before jibs and hydraulics.

Before low loaders most crawlers travelled like this.

One of the Coltman Matadors that Peter drove. Peter Key of Ullesthorpe spent twenty years with Coltmans mainly on Matadors and has kindly arranged these photographs for us.

The Amazing Allis

George Dunnings of Durley, Hants drove this wartime lease lend Allis Chalmers Model U, with auto mower front mounted winch. 250 cube was a fair load for this nice little outfit.

FOR 547 was a 6 LW engined Foden STG 6. She clocked 400,000 miles and I last heard of her, still at work, in East Yorkshire.

This big elm was ex-Beaulieu bound for Stokenchurch, Bucks. Mind the saw George! I once slipped off a jib and sat on a saw like that.

George with the ERF artic he drove.

The Brothers Grove of Tebworth

A lady who showed my daughter Ruth great kindness gave a copy of SORTH to her father. Quite by chance, this man Arthur Edwards worked as a boy for Amos Grove, and held the key to a rare photograph that he featured on. Arthur Edwards walked for miles to peel bark and fell trees and he recalled a regular faller who carried his axes and saws on a solid tyred tricycle. This man and his son travelled Bedfordshire. He would cup his hands to catch the fresh Ash sap and drink it for medicinal purposes. Similarly, Fred Grove, for a sore throat, would chew the gummy resins of fresh felled Larch.

Celebrating the crowning of King George V, powerful Amos Grove strained his heart as anchor man at tug-of-war and never worked again. He and elder son Fred were local undertakers. A ledger shows a complete funeral cost twenty five shillings and the poor paid a penny a week to cover it. Fred saw his future in coffin board manufacture and later, when joined by his younger brother Sidney, they finally produced two hundred coffin sets a week. So Fred's daughter, Miss Ena (to me) reminded me.

Fred was a stickler for punctuality, even his own. Once when slightly late for chapel he turned back home rather than insult the Lord! He had three rules of S's; no smoking, swearing or standing about, and when the one about swearing in the yard went unheeded by a driver delivering a rare electric motor after the war, Fred was so enraged he said: "That's it, take it back." So fanatical was he about these rules, that he refused delivery of this much wanted scarce motor.

In 1946 it was Fred who interviewed me for the Latil driver's job. None of the rules was a problem to me; however, the poorly braked Latil was. Just two wheels on the drug were required to hold all eight, and one needed the trailer if only going to the petrol pump. My regular mate Harry Smith taught me the craft of loading and holding this wandering brute (in common with all Latils) on the road. In return I accepted his skilled practices with the catapult. On entering Tingrith Wood Harry would switch the engine on and off two or three times in order that the ensuing backfire would fool the gamekeeper when he bagged the odd rabbit with his 4/10 gun; hence a permanently split silencer.

At Church Farm, Astwick, a Poplar tree stump was so big all four wheels of a Standard Fordson was driven up on to it. Harry Smith and I carted the tops of this tree. At Shefford I could turn into Ampthill Road with thirty-footers but one slipped back four feet whilst roping out. Arriving at this corner Harry stopped me with the tree end just six inches from the butcher's shop window. Twenty minutes sweat on the cross cut saw, the fallers had thrown away, because I'd run over it, had made little impression when a bobby appeard. Removing helmet, tunic and cycle clips he gave us a blow for half an hour with this distorted 'Diston'. When the traffic flowed again an eager bystander anticipated my fate with the PC. Mopping his brow the constable repeated, "What am I going to do? Tend these blisters. If anyone wants booking it's the inventor of those saws".

I used to dread Ampthill Hill. Crawling up this long drag a blue speck in the Latil driving mirror would be a PC on a bike who would catch us up, dismount, walk past and be at the crossroads on duty before we got there. No wonder John Bunyan featured this as the 'Hill Difficulty' in Pilgrims Progress. Harry used the ensuing forty minutes to execute a number of chores. He would alight, as I dropped down into bottom booster, and place a block near to the near carriage wheel, knowing if the engine died, as it was wont, he had about thirty seconds before the vacuum needle zeroed and we would run back. Weather permitting, he would perch up on a bag of faller's chips situated behind the cab. Having rolled a few fags he would work out the measures, knowing anything over 275 cube spelled trouble. About half way up Harry would grab the radiator brush guard and swing up on to the mudguard, sit down and start topping up with water from a can kept beside the bonnet. For a break Harry would reclimb into the cab and tend to the trophies of the day, like gutting a couple of rabbits or plucking a pheasant, all the time listening for the slightest tone change of the roaring engine. Another regular chore was to remove the flimsy floor board and top up the gear box, long since void of oil seals, thus avoiding gear seizure. At least once he would walk with his head below the cab checking amounts of daylight through the chassis' cracks. There was always the danger this old girl would revert back to her forbears. In 1911 George Latil of Marseille, France built the first front wheel drive vehicle. He next devised an engine, gear box and front axle mounted into a chassis cut in half that would bolt into the shafts and motorize any horse drawn vehicle. His next brainwave was to fix two such half chassis end on, having removed the rear engine, thus gaining the four steering four wheel drive Latil resulting in interchangeable front and rear springs and drives; a design that remained basically the same up to 1955. But I digress. The top of the hill was generally celebrated with a shared swig of cold tea from a Tizer

Arthur Edwards stands proudly beside his father (with axe), wheelright and faller. This huge veneer poplar was felled beside the A5 and with difficulty hauled by horses to Dunstable Station. The London buyer sent back a fine trade sample from it, which was kept in the Grove's office for many years. Sidney Grove, far right, was in charge of this major operation. Courtesy Luton Museum and Art Gallery.

Harry Smith with the FWD. After the Latil this was a dream machine with every facility, even a rifle rack for Harry's 4/10 gun.

bottle, more water for the tractor and a drop of the same to pour over my burning right foot. Finally, back in the yard, any sense of achievement vanished when Sid Grove would question "don't suppose you dare put more on with the hill?"

The Latil ran away with me three times before I sent anonymously for a Unipower catalogue on the Groves' behalf. I was of course not surprised when the brothers confronted me with a brown envelope. "I suppose this is your doing", said Fred whilst his brother went on to explain what £3,000 would buy from Stenners (saws) of Tiverton. Needless to say this brought me no Unipower but an FWD from Vass's of Ampthill, the next best thing.

My old friend Colin Kiteley came to Groves in 1946 and stayed on for forty years working for three companies. He turned his hand to everything; management, hauling, sawing, saw doctoring, crane driving, buying and selling and part time chauffeur. He saw the firm rise to twenty three employees and fall back to one or two. Many post war successes were of Colin's thinking and many were lost due to restraint. Fred confided to Colin that he started with no financial assets, but he bought his first tree by picking and selling gooseberries.

Tough as nails Fred extracted a tooth with my plyers wrapped in a hankie. I declined when he offered me his services. "I'd pay no dentist two and six", he jibed. He was eccentric, yes, but also shrewd and successful. Even at eighty, he could 'cube up' a standing tree with brilliant accuracy, looking through binoculurs, whilst sitting in the car. Together the brothers bought Alder and Lime, from all over the country, to plank for the Luton Hat Block Industry, and they excelled in all English hardwoods. Both men were practising Methodists and did a lot of good by stealth. Their tolerance of my impatience must be recorded, and although not really appreciated at the time, on reflection, they gave me a thorough if rough start in the timber trade.

Round about Chippy

When the railway came to Chipping Norton Tom Stanley's grandfather supplied timber to shore up the tunnel. Tom was 15 years when his father sent him at cordwood cart with their Model T Ford lorry after just one day's tuition. Tom now aged seventy nine had the key to the Chippy timber history.

An estate owner said: "I'm selling my old Buick straight 8 car. That would make a better lorry," and for £34 it did. Tom cut the body off, rear of the front seats, and for four years it carried two tons with ease. They carted 7,000 tons of cordwood from nearby Heythrop Park where Tom came to know C. R. Claridge, Timber Merchants. They made headlines in 1926 with the 'Heythrop Giants'; 75ft long larch trees for ships' masts came into Chippy Station. Loaded two at a time with horse teams they were turning New Street corner (now altered) when the tails jammed on the fence, lifting and then suspending the horse in the shafts high in its harness, until 20ft could be cut off the tails. The RSPCA took Claridges to court for cruelty. From the dock the horseman explained, that his hores only responded to kindness, not cruelty. He asked permission for four of his horses to be brought to the foot of the ten steps, then claimed that with words alone and not touching them he would talk them round the Town's Hall's aisles to demonstrate his point. The court declined, but were so impressed that a token fine of only £1 was made on Claridges.

Two World War 1 FWD's were made into artic units very successfully. Later Foden and Latil were each asked for a demonstration, and an order for four tractors was pending. A trailer with 300 cube was taken to Sunrising Hill, a local bit of natural nasty work. Each tractor had to take the load down and then return. Latil went first, the load pushing them into the hedge half-way down. The Foden did better but twenty yards from the top someone, perhaps intentionally ran out into the road. After wheel spin the Foden got going and landed the order.

Jim Morrell is an ex-Claridge man, and he remembers them having fifteen horses out at Great Tew. He drove a Fowler and their first Cat. RD6. He loaded the first Foden chaindrive diesel driven by Foden's star demonstrator, Tommy Dolan. Claridges also had a sawmill at Exeter. In 1928 at the time when all Devon timbering was rained off, it seems Claridges were still at work. Tractor Traders Ltd., of London, had imported and sold them the first Caterpillar 60 'Logging Cruiser' to go into UK timber work. It weighed nearly 10 tons and waded through deep slurry like no other crawler.

Soon I was out at Milton under Wychwood at Alfred Groves Ltd. They were builders and once when they were slack, a friend on a shoot, suggested Mr. Groves put in an old rackbench to cut a bit of timber. Frank Bolter came to manage the firm in 1947. He was given a free hand and told to do as he liked so long as he made money. His ambitious achievements included buying some of the biggest elm in the country from Cornwall to Scotland, and processing them in the mill he masterminded. He purchased a big Dankart Bandmill that would take a 500 cube tree, and two steam cranes, one of which was later fitted with a Gardner 5LW. These two men had a gentleman's agreement and honoured it to the letter, hence a large and prosperous mill.

For twelve years Brian Gorton of Witney learned his craft from Frank Bolter.

When it comes to 'cubeing up' a standing tree, it shows! Building on lessons learned, Brian became his own man. He talks of his good fortune to have enjoyed the 'golden age' prior to the scourge of DED, when he bought and sold 300,000 cube of timber a year. At one time Brian had eight or nine gangs of fallers and up to thirteen loads of timber on the road in one day. Misfortune came in the form of four or five loads of timber that disappeared from Denham. We've all lost the odd tree, but entire loads, pre-self loading days, is rather cheeky. Long harmonious contracts on big estates like Blenheim, Woburn and Chequers, where he survived three Prime Ministers, say much for his workmanship. He is quick to refer to the back up of drivers like Bernard Berrows and fallers of Don Groom's calibre.

Cricket is the great love of Brian's life. He 'wheedled' a bat from a firm who purchased 600 cube of willow. This bat scored three half centuries when he was privileged to recently tour Australia with Captain R. H. Hawkins XI. 'How's Zat?' for a lad who loves cricket and buying timber equally.

Brian has harvested the mature timbers in Luton Hoo Park for fifteen years. In the midst of my post-cardiac depression, I was invited there, to meet his colleague Pat Stanley, Tom's son. This meeting led to two most important events. The first was an invitation to take a trip with Pat in his Volvo Turbo 12 to Leicester that I recorded and then, with other items, produced a tape, which with donations raised over two thousand pounds for the CORDA heart charity. Secondly, it was while hurtling up the M1 at 60 mph I decided to throw off the malaise of my enforced retirement and make some good use of the days I had been spared. Pat flicked

The first Caterpillar 60 'Logging Cruiser' works in deep slurry and rain, in Devon 1928. The driver says by far the biggest problem was getting all the cans of petrol into the woods for the thirsty petrol engine!

One of Claridges two World War 1 FWD's. Tom Stanley remembers this 325 cube of larch. Blacksmith Otto Zachow USA designed the FWD. His sales pitch being 'whoever saw a mule walk on only two legs'!

through the Volvo gear box as we charged up the long hill to the A6 with 625 cube on the tri axle trailer he had had made up to his own specifications. About forty years ago it used to take me twenty five minutes to ascend this drag with a clapped out Latil and 200 cube top whack. My mate, with his catapult would stalk rabbits in the adjoining fields, appearing from nowhere if the roar of the Latil should falter!

At twenty one years Pat had his hired Neville's AEC 'Mercury' carrying loads best suited to a 'Mammoth'! Many prime elms around Chippy were fifty quarter girth and nine feet diameter. With his Stihl 090 sixty three inch blade Pat felled, then hauled many of them. His record was confirmed by Frank Bolter. A sixty six feet long elm had 752 cube, and when cut in half the first thirty two feet produced nine 12ft × 12ft thirty two feet piles for Dover Harbour.

The last big tree I'm likely to see was a Spanish chestnut, felled beautifully by Don Groom, at Luton Hoo during 1986. It was nine feet diameter, seventy four feet girth, yielding 697 cube of good unshaken timber. Pat quartered the butt as no mill today could take it whole.

A sense of quiet pride prevails in this man's work and his outfit, as seen in the tasteful artistry on the cab of the Scania M112 that now pulls the tri axle trailer.

Hewing the timber for the Chippy Tunnel was an astonishing achievement for Ernest Tom Stanley, the first of many such achievements running down through four generations.

A tri-axle trailer and AEC 'Mercury' tractor. No lack of ambition with young Pat here.

There was 752 cube in this splendid elm. Pat cut the tree then delivered it in one load. The first 32 feet produced nine 12 × 12 pileing baulks, Mr. Bolter told me.

Loaded and leaving for Alfred Groves Ltd. at Milton-Under-Wychwood.

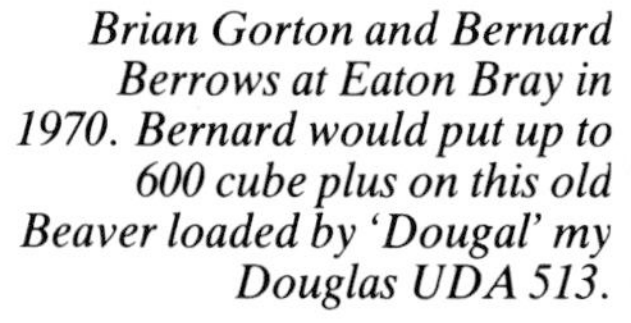

Brian Gorton and Bernard Berrows at Eaton Bray in 1970. Bernard would put up to 600 cube plus on this old Beaver loaded by 'Dougal' my Douglas UDA 513.

Brian, Pat and Allis. Pat's faithful ex-WD British Army Allis Chalmers AEC 505 engined loader.

The Volvo Turbo 12 before setting off to make the Corda Tape that raised £2,000 plus. It was on this day, hurtling up the M1 at 60 mph I threw off my malaise and decided to make good use of the days I have been spared.

The 9 ft. dia. Spanish chestnut Don Groom felled in Luton Hoo Park, 1985.

Pat starts cutting with his Stihl 090. When quartered up there was a 697 cube of good unshaken timber here.

The chestnut leaving the park.

Tony Burns, Executive Director of Corda, presents plaques to Brian Gorton and Pat Stanley for their part in the fund raising. Luton Hoo Park 1986.

Wood and Wurlitzers

The first costly lesson of land clearance came in the form of a big stump, concealed under blackberry scrub amongst trees that I had agreed to grub and clear for a fixed price. A seasoned contractor, named Bill Forth, put in a BT 100 Drott Shovel, saving my face and wallet. Bill employed two red headed twin brothers, John and Dave Tucker, who each operated a Drott with great dexterity. In a third of the time, standing in the Drott bucket. I topped a whole row of poplars fifteen feet high. So economical was this practice that I would hire a Drott on hourly work solely for lopping, long before the days of 'Simon Hoists'. Later, in their own business as Tucker Bros. we grubbed and cleared some of the biggest trees in Beds and Bucks, mostly by pulls from Eunice my Unipower and two Drotts pushing. Brother Fred Tucker orchestrated the action with hand signals. The Drott that didn't back off quickly enough could be overturned in a moment as the massive roots lifted. These lads worked all hours yet were full of pranks, with questions like, did I know lemon trees grew in Britain; and should I get some botanical

Myself and Dave Tucker. A guts-acheing job this rooting. Ash were always 'screwed in tight' but these elm succumbed to the drott with ease.

authority in to see the one I had to fell the next day? Sure enough a medium tree, resembling an ash, certainly was heavy all over with lemons! *Jiffy Lemons* — the product was new at the time and a box full of damaged ones had been found at the tip, but even careful wiring them on to the ash tree made no lemon of 'Moll', as they called me.

Helen and I started an electronic organ business for our eldest daughter who played organs better than chain saws. Eunice towed a mobile studio, with three organs and a generator, around rallies and shows. Tucker Bros., minus their Drotts, carried a big theatre console up the wide stairway of the Swan Hotel for the Leighton Buzzard Fat Stock Show Dinner. We sold the console and never looked back. We founded the first Wurlitzer Organ Club in the UK, which I ran like my Youth Club, selling fun and fellowship. The low powered but high sales technique mystified the Wurlitzer executive whose sole agency we held for many years. This venture closed after twelve years with the advent of our grandchildren.

WHAT NO SAFETY OFFICER? On very wet sites the lads would collect me and my kit in this bucket and track perhaps a mile into the woods.

THE WING PARK GIANT! The biggest oak tree we grubbed. The root measured 16 ft from Dave down below up to John beside me.

Rob Forth digs a hole with their International BT 20 to bury hundreds of roots. In 1957-58 1,120 none productive prune and apple trees were dozed out for W.E. Wallace, The Comp, Eaton Bray. I contracted to cut these up with my Danarm 'Whipper' chainsaw at 9d a tree. I averaged 13 trees to the hour.

'Wurtitzer means music to millions' was emblazoned on Eunice's radiator. Lifting an £850 organ, delivered on a flat lorry, was rather hairy knowng the Unipowers winch brake.

Tom's Treasures

Ten horses double up to bring this huge tree up the hill for Miles & Sons of Stamford. They used horses up to 1956.

Miles had six Clayton Shuttleworth engines. 400 cube on each of the two trailers was the norm, as seen here.

A timber and general Latil (note the coach built forward opening cab doors) later owned by Miles, then Oliver Goff and Whattons.

Twiggdons had several Latils. As showmen their involvement in timber is traced to wartime when their big steamers drove saws for Miles.

Bob Culpin (right) was loading into his seventies. Here, with driver Tom Williamson, they hauled a big oak with root attached. Not busting the drawbar and turn-table was sheer genius. Tom and these wonderful photographs are sadly all that remain of Miles, who used to cut 1,000 coffin sets a week in their heyday.

Here and There

These photographs do not relate to the stories, but are nevertheless unique. I have included them for your added interest.

Happy Days. Circa 1950s

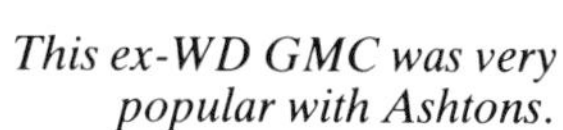

This ex-WD GMC was very popular with Ashtons.

This GMC 6 × 6 would scorch at 60 mph until later fitted with a Perkins P6 that slowed her down a little.

Fowler Engine No.8381. Johnsons Timber Merchants, Hereford. Courtesy of The Jack Turner Collection.

Foden D Type tractor. A & R Williams of Hereford. Courtesy of The Jack Turner Collection.

Driver Eric Pritchard was surprised to find this forester on Unipowers stand, Earls Court, 1956 and drove it home after the show.

Denis Lee with the Foden two stroke which he drove from new. Now beautifully restored and still worked by George Vines, Glous.

Bernard Berrow's father demonstrated Latils. This was a prized photograph. Circa early 1930's.

The concept of the Jensen Tug came from Staussler to Latil UK. After a boardroom row Latil's engineer and demonstrator Mr. Riekie took the idea to Jensons and developed it there.

Perhaps the only remaining Unipower 'Invader' 4 × 4 road site artic. Launched in 1971, a Perkins V8 510 drives an Eton 5 speed gearbox via a 2 speed Thornycroft transfer box, Maudslay axles and a York Big D 5th wheel complete the Motley spec. A few were exported but it was all too late and costly. HLU 428K new to Cross of Southall. Now ballasted, she tows scrapers for contractor Richard Burt, Nr. Towcester, who is well known in all earth moving circles.

One of the many Cat. D4s that speeded our timber industry.

How to "roll" a Latil, and keep cool.

Many remember Derek Petty of Northchurch, Herts. He drove this Foden for Easts of Berkhamstead, and sent this photograph, just before he died, to Bert Winkfield.

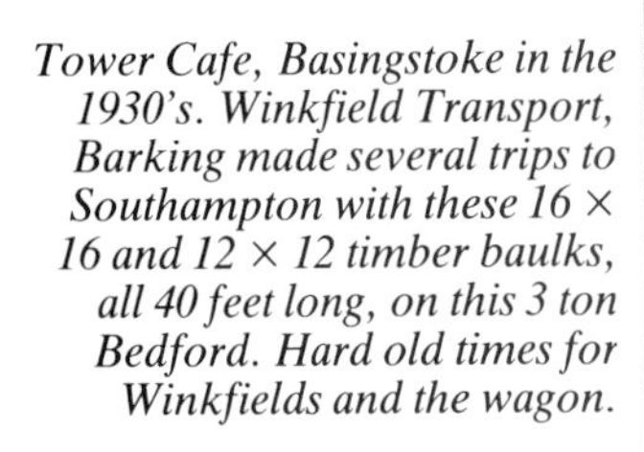

Tower Cafe, Basingstoke in the 1930's. Winkfield Transport, Barking made several trips to Southampton with these 16 × 16 and 12 × 12 timber baulks, all 40 feet long, on this 3 ton Bedford. Hard old times for Winkfields and the wagon.

Montague Meyers Maudslays fill up on the A1.

Enterprising Allan Lloyd of Malvern regularly lops trees with his 100 ft. AEC turntable ladder. Seen here with Roy Finch reducing a beech.

The John Gregory 1958 Unipower, only 18,000 miles on the clock. Photographed by John Cole of Rubery who has rescued and restored several Unipowers for preservation.

The child's truck dates this Timber and General Mark I Latil. 6 wheeled trailers with 600 cube was the norm, but over sized tyres and Perkins R6 engines were all a bit much for these old ladies.

Latil MK I somewhere in Norfolk (note oversize tyres).

No room on top of this Leyland belonging to Ken Tyrrall. Loaded by the County Crawler in Surrey.

They tell me this Marshall spent much of its time on two wheels in Wales.

BTU 101 was a TG5 chain drive Foden, new to A.K. Cooper of Sweffling in 1937 and traded to Latil tractors in 1938. Purchased by T.T. Boughton, this Foden was later entirely rebuilt in their own workshop as a STG 5 shaft drive tractor. A high speed diff made this a superb tractor, operated by Bernard Ruff and Alf Chiltern.

Bob Rose's delightful little ERF 'Betty'. The winch, anchor and jib was all fitted by Bob and are still worked around Whitchurch, Bucks.

Loading in glorious Devon 1940s. Note the 'Spy' time recorder mounted above the winch.

A splendid Foden! Allan and Marlene Lawrence of Oxford own and have kept the original livery of GV 8092. New to Reynolds of Bury St. Edmunds 1941 to 65.

JHK 57H, new to Wood Bros. of Rayleigh, Essex in 1969. This was the very last Unipower timber tractor built. At Clumber Park Reg Wood assured me, she is in first class condition and regular work, as seen here in 1986.

A wartime scene in Hunts. One of the 85 FWD (CU) Cummins engined timber tractors that came over on lease lend, aboard a Montague Meyers ERF.

The author with 'Dougal' his Douglas in the 1970s. Before my root trailer I took 12 massive roots about 10 feet wide on the Douglas jib down through Dunstable to the tip. A slight incline had her rearing up with three of them causing me to winch them 30 yards along a public road aided by friendly policemen, bless em!

This ex-Parkend Sawmill Forest of Dean Unipower, now resides in Scotland.

A very smart International. B & J Davies of Bucknell.

ETS, Danbury, Essex had a fleet of 15 Unipower Type G Foresters, some were leased through the Ministry of Supply Home Timber Control Schemes.

Remember when we really did see Bedfords everywhere?

3 early Latils operated by James Walker Ltd. Longwick, Princes Risborough, circa 1930s.

The Mark 5 handles a 200 ton load with ease. The two applications shown below and bottom demonstrate the tremendous flexibility of the Mark 5 to adapt to your specific loading and hauling needs.

No, not Latimer's Sawmills! I asked our Canadian cousins, Butler Bros, Victoria B.C., about achievements. This 8 wheeler has optional 1,000 H.P. Detroit, Cummins or Cat engines and finger tip control with 200 ton up!! Aclaimed the world's biggest timber transporter! If you know of a larger outfit Butlers probably built that too.

The Great North West!

"These have water cooled brakes and need it out here", wrote a man who went out from Bedfordshire to try his fortunes in lumber. These are just two of some snapshots he sent back.

Achievements in Timber at Eaton Bray

Accepted as the largest Wych elm in the Home Counties, this tree at Yew Tree farm in Eaton Bray, blew over in a gale in 1938. Throughout the war the farmer's daughters Minnie and Letitia (Tish) Sharrett cut up almost the entire tree into logs, working often by lantern at night, since they were at work by day.

In 1954 only the massive crown remained which the writer chain sawed up, watched by the village carpenter, Max Sharrett, who said, "whoever thought they would sharpen the chain of a motorbike and cut wood with it".